Collateralized Debt Obligations

European University Studies
Europäische Hochschulschriften
Publications Universitaires Européennes

Series V
Economics and Management

Reihe V Série V
Volks- und Betriebswirtschaft
Sciences économiques, gestion d'entreprise

Vol./Bd. 3351

PETER LANG
Frankfurt am Main · Berlin · Bern · Bruxelles · New York · Oxford · Wien

Albert Schaber

Collateralized Debt Obligations

First Loss Piece Retention, Combination Notes, and Tranching

PETER LANG
Internationaler Verlag der Wissenschaften

Bibliographic Information published by the Deutsche Nationalbibliothek
The Deutsche Nationalbibliothek lists this publication in the Deutsche Nationalbibliografie; detailed bibliographic data is available in the internet at <http://www.d-nb.de>.

Zugl.: München, Univ., Diss., 2009

D 19
ISSN 0531-7339
ISBN 978-3-631-58795-9

www.peterlang.de

Preface

This doctoral dissertation was written during my time as research assistant at the Institute of Capital Market Research and Finance at Ludwig-Maximilians-University in Munich and accepted in July 2009. Several people contributed to the successful completion of my dissertation, to whom I want to express my appreciation and gratitude.

First and foremost, I would like to thank Professor Bernd Rudolph for being my doctoral advisor. His input and advice throughout the entire process were critical to the success of the dissertation. Also, he gave me a great degree of freedom in pursuing my research and created a fruitful and entirely positive working environment. Furthermore, I would like to thank Professor Andreas Richter for becoming my thesis referee. He highlighted several important aspects of my work and thereby helped to improve the thesis considerably.

I am also indebted to Dr. Marco Krohn and Markus Ernst. They granted me access to different data sources and thus enabled the empirical analyses of this dissertation. I very much enjoyed the stimulating discussions with Marco Krohn and am thankful for his market participant's perspective on my research.

Moreover, I want to thank my former and current colleagues at Ludwig-Maximilians-University Christian Annetzberger, Philipp Gann, Florian Haagen, Florian Habermann, Robert Härtl, Stefanie Hochhold, Bernd Hofmann, Martin Jaron, Philipp Jostarndt, Julia Scholz, Marion Schulz, Beatrice von Sydow and Tea Szabo. Their comments and discussions during doctoral seminars and during everyday work contributed significantly to this thesis. Wiebke Klein and Susanne Müller provided invaluable assistance to all organizational issues.

My parents, my sisters and friends also supported me in this endeavor. I very much appreciate their help and their continuing interest in the progress of my dissertation. Finally, I want to thank my girlfriend Susanne for her invaluable support. It was her exceptional sense of humor that helped me to pass also the hard times during the creation of this work!

Munich, July 2009 | Albert Schaber

Table of Contents

List of Figures . . . 10
List of Tables . . . 12
List of Abbreviations . . . 13
List of Symbols . . . 15

1 Introduction . . . 19
1.1 Motivation . . . 19
1.2 Course of examination and main results . . . 22
Bibliography for chapter 1 . . . 26

2 Selling the first loss piece in CLOs and the role of reputation . . . 29
2.1 Introduction . . . 29
2.2 The decision to securitize assets . . . 31
2.2.1 Raising funds . . . 32
2.2.2 Risk transfer . . . 33
2.2.3 Arbitrage . . . 37
2.3 Security design from an agency perspective . . . 38
2.3.1 Ex ante asymmetries and adverse selection . . . 39
2.3.2 Ex post asymmetries and moral hazard . . . 42
2.3.3 Implications and critical issues . . . 43
2.4 Two models on asset securitization . . . 44
2.4.1 Model 1: Using CLOs to refinance growth opportunities 44
2.4.1.1 Model setup . . . 44
2.4.1.2 Whole sale vs. securitization . . . 47
2.4.1.3 Repeated securitization . . . 50
2.4.2 Model 2: Using CLOs to manage regulatory capital . . . 56

2.4.2.1 Changes to the model setup 56

2.4.2.2 Whole sale vs. securitization under the Basel I regime 59

2.4.2.3 Whole sale vs. securitization under the Basel II regime 63

2.4.2.4 Repeated securitization under the Basel II regime 65

2.5 Discussion of main results and critical issues 68

2.6 Conclusion 72

Appendix for chapter 2 74

Appendix A: Existence of equilibria in the repeated game – model 1 74

Appendix B: Analysis of the repeated game in the regulatory context – model 2 75

Appendix B.1: Derivation of the threshold $\tilde{P}$ 75

Appendix B.2: Existence of equilibria in the repeated game – model 2 76

Bibliography for chapter 2 81

3 Combination notes: Market segmentation and equity transfer . . 87

3.1 Introduction 87

3.2 Derivation of hypotheses on the structuring and impact of combination notes 91

3.3 Data description and combination note properties 93

3.3.1 General descriptive statistics 93

3.3.2 Exploring the properties of combination notes 98

3.4 Empirical analysis of combination notes 100

3.4.1 Determinants for the tranching of combination notes . . 100

3.4.1.1 The benchmark case – tranching of plain vanilla tranches 103

3.4.1.2 Tranching of combination notes 105

3.4.1.3 Tranching of combination notes versus the deal 107

3.4.2 Combination notes and risk transfer 111
3.4.2.1 Measuring equity transfer 111
3.4.2.2 Equity transfer and deal characteristics 112
3.4.2.3 Equity transfer and launch spreads 115
3.5 Conclusion 125
Appendix for chapter 3 127
Bibliography for chapter 3 128

4 Asset pool quality and tranching of CDOs 133
4.1 Introduction 133
4.2 Literature review 134
4.2.1 Theoretical aspects of tranching 134
4.2.2 Existing empirical evidence on tranching 137
4.3 Derivation of a transaction cost-based hypothesis of the number of differently rated tranches 138
4.4 Empirical analysis of asset pool quality and tranching 146
4.4.1 The dataset 146
4.4.2 Available measures of asset pool quality 149
4.4.3 A simulation of the number of differently rated tranches 152
4.4.4 Empirical findings on the tranching decision 156
4.4.5 Empirical findings on the size of the junior and the senior tranche 163
4.5 Robustness of results 167
4.6 Summary of results and discussion 170
4.7 Conclusion 171
Appendix for chapter 4 173
Appendix A: Mean-preserving spread of the loss rate distribution 173
Appendix B: Numerical mapping of ratings 174
Appendix C: Predicted probabilities for the ordered logit analyses 175
Bibliography for chapter 4 177

List of Figures

2.1 Time structure 46

3.1 Actual rating CN vs. CN rating revisited 100

4.1 Variance of loss distribution LHP as function of p and ϱ 141
4.2 LHP density and distribution functions for different values of p and ϱ 145
4.3 Scatterplot of the average rating vs. the lnWARF 150

List of Tables

3.1 Asset manager ratings 94
3.2 Rating distribution 96
3.3 Descriptive statistics on the deal level 97
3.4 Tranching of plain vanilla tranches 104
3.5 Tranching of combination notes 106
3.6 Predicted probabilities for discrete changes in Ln size CN 107
3.7 Tranching of combination notes versus the deal 109
3.8 Equity transfer and deal characteristics 113
3.9 Launch spreads and risk transfer (i) 119
3.10 Launch spreads and risk transfer (ii) 123
3.11 Rating indices and rating agencies' letter grades 127

4.1 Moody's cumulative default rate (one year time horizon) by rating 1920-2004 in % 142
4.2 Summary statistics on the number of tranches 147
4.3 Frequency of rating-jumps 148
4.4 Summary statistics on the S&P measures and correlations, $N = 191$ 152
4.5 Tranching and pool quality – full sample 157
4.6 Tranching and pool quality – univariate analysis of the small sample 159
4.7 Tranching and pool quality – multivariate analysis of the small sample 161
4.8 Junior and senior security and pool quality 165
4.9 Rating indices and rating agencies' letter grades 174
4.10 Predicted probabilities for discrete changes in lnWARF 175
4.11 Predicted probabilities for discrete changes in Spread BBB-AAA 176

4.12 Predicted probabilities for discrete changes in the simulated number of tranches 176

List of Abbreviations

ABS	asset backed securities
BET	binomial expansion technique
C	project C
CAM	CDO asset manager
CDO	collateralized debt obligation
CDS	credit default swap
CFO	collateralized fund obligation
CLN	credit linked note
CLO	collateralized loan obligation
CMBS	commercial mortgage backed security
CN	combination note
C/J	Firla-Cuchra / Jenkinson (2005)
DS	diversity score
EAD	exposure at default
EPDR	expected portfolio default rate (defined by S&P)
FLP	first loss piece
G	growth opportunity
HGB	Handelsgesetzbuch
IAS	International Accounting Standards
IRB	internal ratings-based
LGD	loss given default
LHP	large homogeneous portfolio
LL	leveraged loan
NPV	net present value
O	originator
OAT	obligation assimilable du trésor

OLS	ordinary least squares
RMBS	residential mortgage backed security
SD	standard deviation of portfolio default rate (defined by S&P)
SME	small and medium sized enterprises
S&P	Standard & Poor's
spdef	S&P default measure
spvar	S&P variability measure
SPV	special purpose vehicle
WAL	weighted average life
WARF	weighted average rating factor

List of Symbols

Chapter 2

Symbols used in model 1 and model 2

C	initial investment towards credit C; in model 1 also initial endowment of originator
$F^{H,L}$	high/low asset value of underlying asset credit C
P_{FLP}	price FLP on a stand-alone basis
P_{min}	incentive compatible price for the originator
P_{max}	upper price limit to the investor
V_{e_h,e_l}	repeated game payoff from choosing e_h/e_l
$c(e_{h,l})$	high/low monitoring costs
$e_{h,l}$	high/low level of monitoring by the originator
i	interest rate credit C
r_C	return on credit C
r_f	riskless rate of interest
γ	growth rate of growth opportunity G
δ	discount rate $(1/(1+r_f))$

Specific symbols model 1

P^*	price to be offered by the investor
S	payoff from securitizing the senior security

Specific symbols model 2

$\underline{F^L}$	debtor category specific lower bound for F^L
$G_{Sec}^{BI,BII}$	feasible exposure towards project G in a securitization structure for Basel I/Basel II
$G_{WS}^{BI,BII}$	feasible exposure towards project G in a whole sale structure for Basel I/Basel II
P^{**}	price to be offered by the investor
$\tilde{P}$	threshold for the price to be offered in the repeated game
$rw_C^{BI,BII}$	risk weighting factor credit C for Basel I/Basel II
$rw_G^{BI,BII}$	risk weighting factor project G for Basel I/Basel II

Chapter 4

A	asset value
L	portfolio loss rate
N	number of assets in portfolio
Z	common factor
d	default threshold
p	unconditional probability of default
p_{ij}	joint default probability for two assets
x^*	specific loss rate for intersection of loss distributions
x_i	share of asset i on portfolio
$\Phi(\cdot)$	distribution function of a standard normal variable
$\Phi_2(\cdot,\cdot;\varrho)$	bivariate standard normal distribution function with correlation ϱ
α	parameter of beta distribution
β	parameter of beta distribution
ε	idiosyncratic factor
ρ	default correlation
ϱ	asset correlation

σ^2	variance
σ_{ij}	covariance of two assets

1 Introduction

1.1 Motivation

Several positive attributes have been assigned to asset backed securities (ABS) that help to explain the strong growth of the ABS market segment in recent years. Various types of assets have been securitized until the market growth was finally interrupted by the beginning of the financial crisis in 2007. The securitization of debt instruments such as bonds and loans results in collateralized debt obligations (CDOs), which are at the heart of this thesis and hence are focused on in the following. On the level of individual market participants, several capital market imperfections can be alleviated by the issuance of CDOs or by an investment towards CDOs.[1] From an originator's perspective, the securitization of debt claims can provide an additional, possibly even cheaper, means of funding, as non-marketable assets are transformed into marketable ones, and the quality of the newly created securities is de-linked from the credit risk of the originator. Also, from an originator's perspective, asset securitization can be used as a risk transfer vehicle, be it due to economic or to regulatory reasons. Furthermore, market participants use the technique of securitization to derive market-based prices for credit engagements.[2] To other market participants a CDO is an end in itself, as they try to exploit arbitrage opportunities that arise from the interest payments they collect on the asset side of a transaction and the spreads to be paid on the notes issued by the transaction, hence the liabilities side of the transaction.[3] Investors in CDOs possibly benefit from the access to a new asset class and hence additional diversification opportunities which would

[1] See Roever / Fabozzi (2003) and Rudolph (2005).
[2] See Becker (2007).
[3] See Amato / Remolona (2005) and Brennan / Hein / Poon (2008). The well-established term 'arbitrage transaction' is misleading, as arbitrage-driven transactions encompass risks.

otherwise not be possible, due either to prohibitively high transaction costs or to internal or external investment restrictions.

From a more general perspective, additional benefits have been attributed to modern credit risk transfer instruments such as credit derivatives and securitization. Rule (2001) highlights the benefits of separating the origination of credit from the allocation of the resulting credit risk, which can result in less vulnerable bank portfolios and hence a smoothed credit supply. Also, liquid credit risk transfer markets can generate market prices that can help to improve the allocation of credit risk.[4] However, there are several obstacles to the seamless functioning of credit risk transfer markets and therefore to the realization of systemic benefits of credit risk transfer, which were equally addressed by Rule (2001) and Deutsche Bundesbank (2004). Some threats to the functioning of credit risk transfer markets are addressed in this thesis and therefore lined out shortly in the following.

Generally, investors in ABS face the results of adverse selection as well as moral hazard, as originators can be tempted to repackage below-average quality assets or to shirk on monitoring.[5] Therefore the security design of ABS needs to mitigate these agency conflicts, with a stylized solution for securitization transactions being the retention of the most subordinated claim (the first loss piece, FLP, or equity piece) by the originator, which is comparable to a deductible in insurance contracts.[6] Furthermore there is a high degree of concentration among market participants, especially in the segment of credit derivatives, combined with a general lack of transparency on the distribution of credit risk.[7] Given that credit derivatives are moreover employed in synthetic CDOs, this together implies that credit risk transfer markets are vulnerable to market disturbances.[8] Additionally, the complexity of credit risk transfer products

[4] Deutsche Bundesbank (2004), pp. 36-38 emphasizes the same benefits. See also European Central Bank (2006), pp. 28-30 for a generally positive outlook for the impact of credit risk transfer instruments on banking sector stability.

[5] Agency conflicts are not limited to the investor-originator relation; see for example Ashcraft / Schuermann (2008) for a comprehensive examination of the value chain in securitization with a focus on the subprime mortgage segment.

[6] See among others Gorton / Pennacchi (1995), Riddiough (1997), and DeMarzo (2005).

[7] See Effenberger (2004).

[8] See Rudolph (2007), pp. 12-15.

has increased over time, with examples being the securitization of securitized assets, so-called CDO-squared transactions, or the combination of a share of two or several notes from one securitization transaction to a so-called combination note. This in turn increases the general lack of transparency on credit risk transfer markets.[9] The last aspect to be mentioned is the oligopolistic market structure among rating agencies which is prevalent in the CDO market. The marketability of CDOs is linked to their rating. Rating strongly determines the level of spreads to be paid on a tranche, and hence the attractiveness of a transaction for both investors and the originator.[10] Rating additionally determines the amount of regulatory capital that is tied up for investors that have to comply with Basel II.[11] Market participants as well as regulatory authorities hence collectively rely on the risk modeling techniques of a small number of privately organized companies, which invites the risk of collective misjudgments.

While the above enumeration focuses on CDOs and is not exhaustive, its elements can be identified as causes, among others, for the ongoing financial crisis that has its origin in the segment of securitized US subprime mortgages and that started in 2007.[12] The public issuance of ABS in Europe dropped to about € 55 billion for 2008 from a level of roughly € 530 billion for each of 2006 and 2007, i.e. the financial turmoil almost caused the market for securitized assets to dry up.[13] Nevertheless, market participants still relied strongly on the technique of asset securitization in 2008 in Europe, as a volume of € 600 billion of assets was structured to serve as collateral for the provision of liquidity by central banks. The vast majority of transactions in 2008 were thus not issued publicly but retained.

Given the above illustrated positive properties of credit risk transfer instruments such as CDOs, a smoothly functioning credit risk transfer market is desirable for both individual market participants as well as regulators. The pre-

[9] See Watterson (2005) on institutional issues of CDO-squared and Metayer (2006) on the pricing of CDO-squared.
[10] See Firla-Cuchra (2005).
[11] See Basel Committee on Banking Supervision (2004).
[12] For articles that address causes and remedies concerning the financial crisis see for example Rudolph (2008), Ashcraft / Schuermann (2008), and Franke / Krahnen (2008).
[13] See UniCredit Global Credit Research (2009).

condition for a smoothly functioning credit risk transfer market is a detailed understanding of the various facets of credit risk transfer instruments and market practices. This dissertation addresses three individual aspects of collateralized debt obligations, which have attained only limited attention from academia as well as from market participants but merit closer examination. The three aspects are (i) the ability to sell first loss positions in collateralized loan obligation transactions (CLOs) and the role of issuer reputation, (ii) an in depth analysis of combination notes, and (iii) the relation of asset pool quality and the tranching of CDOs. The findings on these three issues have implications for possible regulatory changes but equally for actions to be taken by market participants aimed at supporting the credit risk transfer market, which highlights the relevance of this thesis. It is hoped that my analysis can help to revive the credit risk transfer market, especially the market for CDOs. The following section illustrates my approach to each of these specific aspects of CDOs, including a short summary of the main results.

1.2 Course of examination and main results

In this dissertation I study three different aspects of collateralized debt obligations, which are analyzed and presented in chapters 2 to 4. All three research questions have been addressed on a stand-alone basis, so that any chapter can be read individually. However, the three topics are closely related and exhibit various connections. Given their close relation, there are some redundancies among chapters 2 to 4, in particular for the respective literature reviews.

In chapter 2 I analyze the ability of an originator of a CLO transaction to sell the first loss piece from a theoretical perspective. To prepare the theoretical analysis, the chapter begins with an illustration of the motives that drive asset securitization in general and CLOs in particular. This includes a short summary of the regulatory framework and some general remarks on the various specifications of CDOs. Thereafter, I review the literature on security design. Given this more general character of the first two sections of chapter 2, they equally serve as a foundation for chapters 3 and 4 of the thesis. The theoretical analysis is laid out in section 2.4. I specifically focus on true sale CLOs as the parties involved in different types of securitization transactions vary, as do their incentives. The only parties involved in my analysis are an originator and an investor. The originator can be thought of as a relationship lender from a bank-based financial system. As mentioned above, an investor in a CLO suffers from moral hazard in case the value of the underlying asset pool is a function of the originator's unobservable monitoring effort. Moreover, an investor in a CLO is exposed to adverse selection, as the originator is tempted to select below-average quality assets ex ante. Existing literature mainly suggests retaining the FLP either to generate adequate incentives for monitoring in the moral hazard setting or as a quality signal in the adverse selection setting. While the retention of first loss pieces was common market practice during the emergence of the market, selling the FLP became more common in recent years, with a major driver being the new regulatory framework Basel II.[14] Models that principally allow for the sale of the FLP are those brought forward by Boot / Thakor (1993) and Plantin (2004). However, they are both based on the existence of sophisticated market participants. I instead focus on reputation effects in chapter 2 and use a repeated game to show that selling the FLP is possible without the creation of distorting incentives for monitoring in a moral hazard setting. Given the main objectives that drive CLO transactions, I formulate the model for two cases, one where a CLO is used to raise funds, and the other where a CLO is used to free up regulatory capital. Selling the FLP without incurring agency costs is possible in both settings; the equilibrium relies on the originator's long-term interest in the ability to sell the FLP. Originators that act according to a short-term horizon must retain the FLP to avoid agency cost in case the moral hazard conflict is severe. Chapter 2 concludes with several hypotheses for empirical research that can be tested once sufficient transparency on the whereabouts of first loss positions is established.

Even though selling first loss positions has become more common in CDO markets, the market for first loss positions is non-transparent and the distribu-

[14] Becker (2006) reports an increasing degree of CLO equity transfer for the German capital market for the year 2005. Watterson (2005), p. 3 reports that there were CDO-squared transactions investing in CDO equity at least since 1998 in the US.

tion of equity pieces largely unknown.[15] Chapter 3 sheds some light on this opaque market by means of an empirical analysis of a particular type of notes issued in CDO transactions: combination notes. Combination notes are formed by combining parts of two or more tranches of a CDO transaction, where one part usually consists of a share of the first loss piece. Hence, deals that comprise combination notes are an object of investigation for which equity transfer, at least to a certain extent, is observable. For the analysis I make use of unique data on 126 European CDOs containing 1385 tranches, thereof 398 combination notes. It is analyzed whether combination notes are purely demand-driven, or whether combination notes also appear to be structured to enable equity transfer. Results indicate that market segmentation strongly determines the structuring of combination notes, but risk transfer objectives seem to be catered by combination notes as well. Further, I analyze whether the observed equity transfer via combination notes has an impact on the pricing of the ordinary tranches of each deal. It is found that a higher degree of observed equity transfer reduces the spread on the ordinary tranches of a deal, which indicates that the existence of FLP investors is a positive sign for market participants.

Chapter 4 examines the relation of the quality of an underlying asset pool and its tranching in CDOs. Theoretical predictions on the number of differently rated tranches in securitization transactions are comparably weak, as the security design literature mainly relies on a two-security structure comprising a senior and a subordinated note. Empirical findings by Firla-Cuchra / Jenkinson (2005) and by Franke / Weber (2007) on the relation of asset pool quality and tranching are mixed. Results of the former indicate an increasing number of differently rated tranches with increasing asset pool quality. Results of the latter indicate an increasing number of differently rated tranches with an increasing default probability, but equally an increasing number with an increasing diversification of the underlying asset pool. Generally, asset pool quality determines the shape of the loss distribution for the underlying asset pool, which should be expected to have a large and unambiguous impact on the tranching of

[15] See Fitch Ratings (2008) for a proposal to increase transparency on the distribution of first loss positions.

a transaction. Given the limited existing evidence, I derive a simple transaction cost-based hypothesis on tranching and predict the number of differently rated tranches to be the higher the lower the quality of the underlying asset pool. I verify this hypothesis empirically for a dataset of overall 805 European CDO transactions using measures of asset pool quality which have not been considered so far in empirical research, as well as a simulation. Results support the transaction cost-based hypothesis on tranching. The results furthermore indicate that actual market conditions on the CDO market have a strong impact on the tranching decision, with less differently rated tranches being issued the higher the actual level of launch spreads on the CDO market.

This dissertation contributes to the extant literature in several ways. First, it increases the understanding of agency conflicts inherent in asset securitization by exploring an alternative mechanism that can explain the sale of first loss positions of CLOs despite moral hazard. Second, this thesis contains the first analysis of deals that comprise combination notes and thus enhances the understanding of complex credit risk transfer instruments. The descriptive statistics of chapter 3 increase market transparency to some extent as the degree of overall equity transfer via combination notes is estimated. The empirical analysis reveals a strongly segmented demand for combination notes. Furthermore, market participants assign a positive value to the existence of equity piece investors, which can also be seen as an indication that market participants account for transparency. Finally, this dissertation sheds light on the role of financial engineering for CDOs and therefore also on the role of rating practices. The results found on the relation of asset pool quality and tranching indicate that the tranching of CDOs is to a large extent determined by financial engineering. This highlights the importance of a proper calibration of input parameters and thus also the risk of relying strongly on a small number of rating agencies and their assessment of input parameters and modeling choices.

Bibliography for chapter 1

Amato, Jeffery / Remolona, Eli (**2005**): The pricing of unexpected credit losses, Working Paper No. 190, Bank for International Settlements, Basel.

Ashcraft, Adam / Schuermann, Til (**2008**): Understanding the securitization of subprime mortgage credit, Federal Reserve Bank of New York, Staff Report no. 318.

Basel Committee on Banking Supervision (**2004**): International convergence of capital measurement and capital standards – A revised framework, Basel.

Becker, Claas (**2006**): Transfer mittelständischer Kreditrisiken, in: *Zeitschrift für das gesamte Kreditwesen*, Vol. 21, pp. 1151–1153.

Becker, Claas (**2007**): Kapitalmarktorientierte Preisbildung für illiquide Mittelstandskredite, in: *Zeitschrift für das gesamte Kreditwesen*, Vol. 14, pp. 721–724.

Boot, Arnoud / Thakor, Anjan (**1993**): Security design, in: *Journal of Finance*, Vol. 48, pp. 1349–1378.

Brennan, Michael / Hein, Julia / Poon, Ser-Huang (**2008**): Tranching and pooling, Working Paper, UCLA.

DeMarzo, Peter (**2005**): The pooling and tranching of securities: A model of informed intermediation, in: *Review of Financial Studies*, Vol. 18, pp. 1–35.

Deutsche Bundesbank (**2004**): Instrumente zum Kreditrisikotransfer: Einsatz bei deutschen Banken und Aspekte der Finanzstabilität, Monatsbericht April 2004.

Effenberger, Dirk (**2004**): Kreditderivate: Wirkung auf die Stabilität der Finanzmärkte, Deutsche Bank Research.

European Central Bank (**2006**): EU banking sector stability, Frankfurt a.M., November 2006.

Firla-Cuchra, Maciej (2005): Explaining launch spreads on structured bonds, Working Paper, University of Oxford.

Firla-Cuchra, Maciej / Jenkinson, Tim (2005): Security design in the real world: Why are securitization issues tranched?, Working Paper, University of Oxford.

Fitch Ratings (2008): Exposure draft: Retaining equity piece risk – Enhancing transparency, New York.

Franke, Günter / Weber, Thomas (2007): Wie werden Collateralized Debt Obligation-Transaktionen gestaltet?, in: *Schmalenbachs Zeitschrift für betriebswirtschaftliche Forschung*, Vol. 57/7 (Sonderheft), pp. 95–123.

Franke, Günter / Krahnen, Jan Pieter (2008): The future of securitization, CFS Working Paper No. 2008/31.

Gorton, Gary / Pennacchi, George (1995): Banks and loan sales: Marketing nonmarketable assets, in: *Journal of Monetary Economics*, Vol. 35, pp. 389–411.

Metayer, Benoit (2006): CDO^2, correlation, overlap, and subordination: Implication for pricing and risk management, in: *Journal of Structured Finance*, Vol. 11, pp. 59–70.

Plantin, Guillaume (2004): Tranching, Working Paper, Tepper School of Business, Pennsylvania.

Riddiough, Timothy (1997): Optimal design and governance of asset-backed securities, in: *Journal of Financial Intermediation*, Vol. 6, pp. 121–153.

Roever, Alexander / Fabozzi, Frank (2003): A primer on securitization, in: *Journal of Structured & Project Finance*, Vol. 9, pp. 5–19.

Rudolph, Bernd (2005): Risikotransferinstrumente und Unternehmensfinanzierung, in: *Schmalenbachs Zeitschrift für betriebswirtschaftliche Forschung*, Vol. 57, pp. 176–181.

Rudolph, Bernd (2007): Kreditrisikotransfer – Abbau alter gegen Aufbau neuer Risiken?, in: *Kredit und Kapital*, Vol. 40, pp. 1–16.

Rudolph, Bernd (2008): Lehren aus den Ursachen und dem Verlauf der internationalen Finanzkrise, in: *Schmalenbachs Zeitschrift für betriebswirtschaftliche Forschung*, Vol. 60, pp. 713–741.

Rule, David (2001): The credit derivatives market: Its development and possible implications for financial stability, Financial Stability Review: June 2001, Bank of England.

UniCredit Global Credit Research (2009): Securitization market watch, as of January 15, 2009, Munich.

Watterson, Paul (2005): The evolution of the CDO squared, in: *Journal of Structured Finance*, Vol. 11, pp. 6–12.

2 Selling the first loss piece in CLOs and the role of reputation

2.1 Introduction

The securitization of assets began in the 1970s with the securitization of mortgages. In the last decade, asset securitization showed a tremendous growth with various assets being securitized until the subprime crisis emerged.[1] In a securitization transaction several assets are combined in a pool and serve as collateral for securities that are issued to investors (asset backed securities ABS). The analysis derived in this chapter specifically focuses on agency conflicts that arise in securitization transactions between originators and investors.[2] Furthermore, the focus is set on true sale CLOs, i.e. the securitization of bank loans, therefore the results must not necessarily apply to other types of securitization as agency conflicts other than the moral hazard conflict lined out in the following might be of considerable importance.[3] In a true sale CLO bank loans are pooled by the originating bank and transferred to a special purpose vehicle.

[1] Assets include residential and commercial mortgages (RMBS, CMBS), credit card receivables, automobile loans, receivables from goods and services, loans and bonds (CDOs), and lately also funds (CFOs). For an early introduction to ABS see Bhattacharya / Fabozzi (1996), for an introduction to ABS in German see Rudolph et al. (2007), chapter 3. For an introduction to CLOs see Jobst (2002) and to CFOs see Fitch Ratings (2002). Market data on ABS transactions is regularly published on platforms like the *European Securitisation Forum* or by industry associations like the *Securities Industry and Financial Markets Association* (formerly the *Bond Market Association*). A similar trend can be identified in the insurance industry with the emergence of catastrophe bonds. See Nell / Richter (2004) for an analysis of the optimal mix of index-linked catastrophe bonds and reinsurance to cover catastrophic risk for a primary insurer.

[2] Franke / Krahnen (2008) focus on compensation schemes and hence the manager-shareholder relation in their simulation-based analysis.

[3] To take an example, an asset manager of a managed CDO who holds a subordinated claim in the transaction might have incentives for risk shifting comparable to the owner-manager raising debt capital analyzed by Jensen / Meckling (1976).

Thereafter, different securities are issued, which offer different claims to the underlying asset pool, with the principle of subordination usually being applied. This restructuring of financial claims however gives rise to two major agency conflicts. First, the originator will be tempted to choose a poor average asset quality for the underlying asset pool, which bears the risk of adverse selection and hence market failure. Second, investors of a CLO face moral hazard in case the value of the asset pool is a function of the originator's unobservable monitoring activity. Depending on the level of subordination, investors of a CLO tranche are exposed to a share of the default risk of the asset pool.[4] This risk transfer reduces the originator's incentive to monitor the relevant claims and thus reduces the expected value of the pool. These agency conflicts were addressed in several articles focusing on the optimal security design. One stylized result of most of the articles is the suggestion to retain the junior tranche (first loss piece (FLP), equity piece) in order to either send an appropriate signal to the market concerning the asset pool quality in an adverse selection setting or to provide the originator with the required incentives to mitigate moral hazard. However, in the CDO market, selling the FLP or parts of the FLP became a common industry practice.[5] The analysis in this chapter tries to provide an economic rational for this observation by developing a simple model of asset securitization, where the focus is set on a moral hazard framework and where two different transaction motives are taken into account.

The remainder of the chapter is organized as follows. First, bank benefits due to asset securitization are lined out. The motives of a bank to securitize assets can be manifold and include funding and risk transfer needs as well as speculative motives. A more profound understanding shall therefore be established in section 2.2. Thereafter, existing literature on the security design is reviewed in section 2.3, where the focus is set on agency-theoretical approaches. In section

[4] Additionally, investors are exposed to interest rate and currency risk in a true sale transaction. As these parameters are exogenous factors they will not be considered below.

[5] See International Monetary Fund (2006), p. 56, Fitch Ratings (2005), p. 6, Watterson (2005) and Becker (2006). Generally, the extent to which equity pieces have been sold is so far unknown to regulators but of considerable interest to them. First empirical evidence can be found in the third chapter of this thesis. Fitch issued a proposal for more transparency concerning FLP retention in June 2008, see Fitch Ratings (2008).

2.4, two simple models on asset securitization are developed. Model 1 is driven by refinancing needs, model 2 by regulatory constraints. It will be shown that an originating bank can sell the FLP without losing the incentives for adequate monitoring. Section 2.5 presents the key results of the analysis and a discussion of critical issues. Section 2.6 concludes with testable hypotheses.

2.2 The decision to securitize assets

If financial markets were perfect and complete the repackaging of financial assets could not add value to a firm. But market frictions exist, which can make asset securitization value generating, where the focus is set on the originator's point of view in the following. Benefits to investors of ABS, which shall not be discussed in greater detail, include the access to certain assets which might otherwise not be possible and which can result in additional diversification of the investor's portfolio.[6] Benefits arising from asset securitization to an originator can be grouped in three categories. First, funding objectives can drive asset securitization. Second, asset securitization can be a result of economic and/or regulatory risk transfer needs. Third, the securitization of assets can be motivated by the exploitation of arbitrage opportunities, which possibly arise from the restructuring of financial claims. As refinancing and risk transfer motives are associated to the balance sheet, transactions pursuing such goals are called balance sheet transactions, while transactions purely driven by arbitrage opportunities are called arbitrage transactions. However, also balance sheet transactions can lead to arbitrage profits. While several transaction motives can be addressed in one deal the three main transaction drivers defined above are lined out separately in the following.

[6] See Bluhm / Overbeck / Wagner (2003), pp. 260-263, Merchant (2004), and Benzschawel / Fok (2006) for an introduction to the investor's point of view on asset securitization and for possible diversification benefits of FLP investments. ABS help to complete capital markets by creating or singling out new cash flow profiles, see Gaur / Seshadri / Subrahmanyam (2003). Note that the benefits to risk shedders, which will be highlighted below, apply vice versa to risk takers.

2.2.1 Raising funds

One motive of securitization is the provision of liquidity to the originator of the transaction, hence, only funded transactions can be employed in that context. However, not every funded transaction provides necessarily liquidity to the originator. Synthetic transactions often are partially funded. The proceeds from CLNs (credit linked notes) usually employed in a synthetic structure remain at the bankruptcy remote SPV (special purpose vehicle) to be reinvested in collateral assets (e.g. default free treasury notes) and thus do not provide liquidity to the originator.[7] Liquidity can be generated by employing a true sale structure.[8] The provision of liquidity by means of securitization can per se be advantageous. First, formerly illiquid asset can be transferred into tradable securities, which adds a new funding source and therefore enhances a bank's flexibility.[9] Second, refinancing via a true sale can be cheaper than alternative means of refinancing. This is especially the case when the spread on the securities issued in the ABS structure is below the spread which the bank would have to pay to the market (money or capital market) due to its own risk profile. Hence, refinancing via true sale is particularly interesting to financial institutions with low credit ratings. This is due to the fact that the spread on the ABS tranches is mainly determined by the quality of the underlying asset pool. Appropriate structuring can result in high ratings of senior tranches and allow financing at comparably low costs. However, if the originator also acts as servicer, some risk of the structure is still associated with the originator (servicer risk) and accounted for by investors.[10] The cash receipts from a true sale transaction can

---

7 The advantage of such a structure is to eliminate counterparty risk for the funded part of the transaction.

8 Funding objectives were the main driver for the first transactions in the securitization market, see Bluhm / Overbeck (2007), p. 185.

9 Some market participants might only be able to invest in investment grade securities due to regulatory or internal constraints. The creation of low risk tranches can therefore enhance the range of potential financiers.

10 The servicer is responsible for the collection of payments and tracks the performance of the collateral assets. A servicer in weak condition or servicer default combined with potential difficulties in finding a new service agent can lead to higher delinquencies and also losses. Rating agencies recently adjusted their methodologies for CDOs to better account for servicer risk. See for example Fitch Ratings (2006).

be utilized for different purposes. The originator can reduce liabilities, leading to a contraction of the balance sheet. Alternatively, the originator can engage in new investment projects resulting in an acceleration of asset turnover on the asset side without a need to undertake changes on the liabilities side of the balance sheet. Furthermore, reinvestment of the cash receipts as well as the reduction of liabilities can both improve financial ratios of the originator.[11]

2.2.2 Risk transfer

From a risk management perspective, regulatory and economic objectives have to be distinguished. Compliance with regulatory capital requirements as well as internal risk management objectives can require the transfer of credit risk. Securitization, synthetic or true sale, is a common instrument enabling risk transfer.[12]

Economic credit risk transfer needs depend on the actual risk distribution in the originator's credit portfolio, which can either make shedding (going short) credit risk or taking (going long) credit risk the appropriate choice. Tranching, which is the predominant structural element of securitization transactions, allows to create claims to specific parts of the risk distribution of the underlying asset pool, which then can be sold to investors or be retained by the originator. Thereby, risk transfer is achieved even if subordinated tranches are retained by the originator as extreme outcomes (tail events) are borne by mezzanine and possibly by senior tranche holders, depending on the severity of the loss event.[13] Furthermore, securitization can not only be employed to change the overall exposure to default risk of a financial institution, but also to reduce the volatility of the profit and loss statement.[14] The effect of securitization on economic capital, commonly defined as the difference between the credit value at

[11] See Ohl (1994), pp. 240-252.

[12] A building block of synthetic CDOs are credit derivatives (especially credit default swaps), which naturally can be employed for credit risk transfer objectives on a stand-alone basis. Traditional credit risk transfer instruments include credit insurance contracts, loan sales, and loan syndication.

[13] See Bluhm / Overbeck (2007), pp. 175-176 for an illustration. Krahnen (2005) points out that an allocation of senior tranches outside the financial sector is vital for its stability.

[14] See Paul (1994), p. 272 and Ricken (2007), pp. 124-128 and the reference therein.

risk at a specified confidence level and the expected loss, depends on the assets chosen for securitization and upon which tranches are transferred to investors. Furthermore, the composition of the overall portfolio needs to be considered, as securitizing a subportfolio results in a change in correlation structures within the remaining credit portfolio and can therefore even increase economic capital. Thus, effects of asset securitization on economic capital cannot be generalized but require a case by case analysis. A side effect of regular participation in the CLO market is that originators can use information acquired in that market for a market based pricing approach of generally non-marketable assets, such as loans to small and medium-sized companies.[15]

Considering the regulatory point of view, the stability of a bank depends on both the riskiness of its assets and the availability of capital that is disposable to cover associated risks. The general principle of the Basel accord is that the ratio of regulatory capital to risk weighted assets has to exceed a minimum threshold that was fixed at 8%. The components of regulatory capital were defined in the first Basel accord[16], and largely still apply under the revised framework Basel II.[17] Significant changes in the new regulatory framework concern the determination of risk weighted assets. Under the first Basel accord, risk weightings were constant across rating categories, and only varied in terms of debtor categories. Roughly speaking, risk weightings were at 0% for sovereigns, 20% for banks, and 100% for corporates. Under the new regulatory framework risk weightings are rating-based and hence risk sensitive. Furthermore, depending

[15] See Becker (2007) for a short description of the approach taken by Deutsche Bank.

[16] The first Basel accord, namely "International Convergence of Capital Measurement and Capital Standards", was published in July 1988 by the Basel Committee on Banking Supervision. Regulatory capital consists of tier 1 capital and tier 2 capital. Tier 1 capital mainly comprises shareholders' equity, tier 2 capital comprises reserves, subordinated debt and other kinds of long-term capital (other than tier 1 equity). Tier 2 capital is limited to 100% of tier 1 capital. See Basel Committee on Banking Supervision (1988), §§ 12-27.

[17] The new regulatory framework "International Convergence of Capital Measurement and Capital Standards – A Revised Framework" was published in June 2004 by the Basel Committee on Banking Supervision and was adopted as the Capital Requirements Directive in June 2006 on the European level, comprising the Directives 2006/48/EC and 2006/49/EC. For German banks, Basel II had to be implemented with the beginning of 2007, however with a grace period until the year-end. For the actual composition of regulatory capital see Basel Committee on Banking Supervision (2004), §§ 41-43 and the references therein, and Commission of the European Communities (2008) for a specification concerning hybrid capital.

on the relevant approach, Basel II allows banks to use internal risk assessments for the determination of their risk weighted assets.[18] As a result, risk weightings for existing loan exposures can change significantly. To take an example, a loan to a AAA-rated corporation required 8% of regulatory capital under Basel I. The amount of regulatory capital is reduced to 1,6% when working with the standard approach of the new capital accord.[19]

Assuming that regulatory capital is a scarce resource that determines the ability of the regulated entities to undertake investment opportunities, freeing up regulatory capital can be value enhancing. Both, the transfer of assets off the balance sheet via true sale, as well as synthetic transactions, allow to free up regulatory capital. Whereas the new regulatory accord comprises detailed rules concerning the treatment of securitization transactions, the old accord did not and opened opportunities for regulatory capital arbitrage.[20] With Basel I high quality assets tied up disproportionately high amounts of regulatory capital, which set the incentive to sell high quality assets while retaining low quality assets. Even though first loss positions had to be deducted completely from regulatory capital under the old regulatory framework, securitizing high quality assets could still be advantageous.[21] The new regulatory framework mitigates these distorting incentives, as high quality assets, due to risk-adjusted weight-

[18] The Basel framework distinguishes the standardised approach and two internal ratings-based approaches, the foundation approach and the advanced approach, see Basel Committee on Banking Supervision (2004). In general, the new regulatory accord provides incentives to implement the advanced internal ratings-based (IRB) approach, as the amount of regulatory capital required for a credit portfolio will, ceteris paribus, be lowest under the advanced IRB approach. Hence, regulatory authorities provide incentives to establish sophisticated risk management facilities (which are necessary to be eligible for the advanced IRB approach) at the regulated entities.

[19] The risk weighting for AAA-rated corporate debtors is at 20% in the standard approach. See Basel Committee on Banking Supervision (2004), § 66.

[20] See Basel Committee on Banking Supervision (2004), §§ 538-643 for the treatment of securitization transactions. For a comprehensive review of the old and the new Basel accord focusing on the treatment of securitization transactions see Emse (2005).

[21] Regulatory capital arbitrage for a portfolio of corporate loans was possible, when the position to be retained was smaller than 8% of the underlying portfolio. If, for example, a transaction could be structured such that the FLP was 4% of the underlying asset pool, the amount of required regulatory capital could be reduced by half in case all tranches except the FLP were sold. However the lion's share of risks associated with the underlying asset pool was retained in such a structure. For the treatment of retained equity positions under Basel I for German banks see Emse (2005), p. 18, and Bundesaufsichtsamt für das Kreditwesen (2002),

ings, require significantly lower amounts of regulatory capital. Therefore, transferring high quality assets, or the risk associated with high quality assets, does not lead to the same capital relief as under the old regulatory accord. Under the new accord, the FLP still needs to be fully deducted from regulatory capital, i.e. the FLP experiences a risk weighting of 1250%. As selling high quality assets does no longer provide an above average relief in regulatory capital, selling more junior tranches including the FLP becomes more attractive as a means of transferring credit risk and thus freeing up regulatory capital. Moreover, similar to economic capital requirements, regulatory capital requirements can be smoothed by means of securitization. Credit assets can experience rating changes that, in case of downgrades, increase capital requirements. Securitizing a share of all assets reduces the volatility of regulatory capital requirements especially when subordinated tranches are sold.

Due to the actual financial crisis, triggered by deteriorations in securitized subprime mortgages, however the risk transfer possibilities inherent in securitization transactions will likely by constrained by financial regulators in the European Union. In October 2008 the European Commission published, after a public consultation, a proposal for amendments to the Capital Requirements Directive, which comprises additional rules concerning securitization.[22] It is intended that originators (or sponsors in case of CDOs) retain a vertical slice of any securitization transactions of at least 5% from the beginning of January 2011 (the originator/sponsor must hold "5 per cent in positions having the same risk profile as the one the credit institution is exposed to"[23], where credit institution refers to the investor). Thus, at least 5% of any tranche will have to be retained when the amendment becomes effective. Further, it is intended that investors have to secure that originators/sponsors maintain at least the minimum economic interest of 5%, so that equally non-EU originators/sponsors are subject to this requirement when approaching European investors. Additionally,

for British banks see Financial Services Authority (2001), Section SE, part 9.6.2, p. 5. For a general review of regulatory capital arbitrage opportunities under Basel I see Jones (2000).

[22] See Commission of the European Communities (2008), pp. 32-34. Note that the following paragraph illustrates the status quo at the time this chapter was written. Therefore, changes to the proposed amendments could have possibly occurred.

[23] See Commission of the European Communities (2008), p. 32.

investors have to prove their ability in assessing securitized structures, and data requirements are outlined. The latter might especially impose a burden to the securitization of securitized positions such as CDO-squared structures, as data requirements are always targeted at the underlying assets, and thus comprehensive for CDO-squared structures. Due to its so far non-binding nature and due to the fact that a 5% retention of the risk profile of any tranche does not necessarily mitigate the moral hazard conflict that is central to this analysis, the 5% vertical retention is not integrated in the model derived below.

Summarizing the above, the FLP plays an important role from the risk management perspective. Economically, the FLP carries a significant share of the underlying risks. Taking the regulatory perspective, the FLP ties up a high amount of regulatory capital when retained. Having the possibility to sell the FLP is hence of high importance to market participants either facing a shortage of regulatory capital and/or intending to transfer significant amounts of credit risk, with these two aspects being closely aligned for the new regulatory accord.

2.2.3 Arbitrage

The third reason for asset securitization mentioned above is arbitrage. Usually, the collateral pool for an arbitrage driven transaction is specifically assembled by the collateral manager and does not consist of assets from an originator's balance sheet.[24] Therefore, arbitrage driven transactions are illustrated only briefly.

Asset managers of arbitrage driven transactions speculate on spread differences of collateral assets on a single asset level and on a portfolio level. While assets are, on the asset side of the transaction, assembled on a single asset basis and interest payments collected asset by asset, the liability side of an arbitrage CDO pays interest on a portfolio level to tranche investors. Market data suggests that spreads paid on bonds are significantly higher than the relevant expected losses.[25] In case idiosyncratic risk could be diversified completely

[24] See Bluhm / Overbeck (2007), pp. 178-184 and the references cited therein for a detailed description of an arbitrage CDO.

[25] See Amato / Remolona (2005), pp. 3-4 and Elton et al. (2001).

in a pool of bonds, retaining the expected loss from that collateral pool would be sufficient to create a riskless senior security. In that case, the originator's arbitrage profit would be the spread collected on the collateral pool less the expected loss and less the spread to be paid on the liabilities side of the transaction. However, evidence suggests that completely diversified portfolios are not attainable in practice so there is risk associated with "arbitrage" CDOs and the term arbitrage might somehow be misleading.[26] In case fully diversified portfolios cannot be achieved, unexpected losses remain, which reduce potential gains from arbitrage transactions. Brennan / Hein / Poon (2008) find that arbitrage is possible as investors fully rely on rating agencies' assessments, which can be exploited by collateral managers, especially in case ratings are based on probabilities of default only.

2.3 Security design from an agency perspective

In order to realize the benefits of asset securitization, potential conflicts, arising due to information asymmetries, need to be addressed when structuring the securities. As already lined out in the introductory section, two major agency conflicts arise due to information asymmetries.

Ex ante, there can be uncertainty concerning the quality of the asset pool. In case investors are not able to observe asset quality ex ante, originators are tempted to select assets of below-average quality and to sell them at the average price. Investors should anticipate the opportunistic behavior and reduce the price they are willing to pay or even retreat from the market resulting in market failure. While this mechanism apparently did not apply during the time period of rapid growth of the ABS market—which is closely associated to the originate-to-distribute model of originators—it now applies all the more during the financial crisis. Therefore, appropriate security design has to enable the originator to credibly commit to selecting average quality assets for the underlying asset pool ex ante.

[26] See Amato / Remolona (2005), pp. 12-20.

Ex post, investors of a CLO face moral hazard as an originator may no longer provide the optimal monitoring effort. Considering for example a relationship lender, monitoring efforts are assumed to be valuable but difficult to observe.[27] In case an originator is no longer exposed to the risk of financial claims due to securitization, but carries the cost of monitoring, he is likely to reduce his effort. Investors, being aware of the potential for opportunistic behavior, will adjust the price they are willing to pay resulting in agency costs. Hence, appropriate security design furthermore has to mitigate the moral hazard conflict inherent in securitization in order to avoid agency costs.

Several articles analyze the optimal security design from an agency perspective given a specific transaction motive and shall be reviewed shortly in the following.

2.3.1 Ex ante asymmetries and adverse selection

Articles focusing on ex ante asymmetries include Boot / Thakor (1993), Riddiough (1997), DeMarzo (2005), and Plantin (2004).

Boot and Thakor (1993) analyze an originator who has private information on the quality of his future cash flows. Some market participants are able to discover the value of future cash flows at some cost while others are not. Boot and Thakor show that it is profitable for the originator to set up an informationally sensitive and an informationally insensitive security. The true value of the informationally insensitive security is public and, therefore, information collection not profitable on that security. Contrary, for the informationally sensitive security information production is profitable. Capable traders will therefore collect information on the sensitive security and be willing to pay a price close to the true value. Pooling several high quality assets can further increase the payoff for high quality originators, as asset volatility can be reduced, making the signal to capable traders less noisy. Boot and Thakor's analysis is supply driven; revenues to the originator are maximized by a security design which induces capable traders to produce information. Boot and Thakor do not focus on se-

[27] Elsas / Krahnen (2004) review relevant literature with a special focus on Germany and the typical "Hausbank" relationship for small and medium-sized firms.

curitization only. In fact, they provide a very general analysis which equally applies to the creation of debt (informationally insensitive) and equity claims (informationally sensitive). Therefore, none of the specific motives for asset securitization mentioned above are explicitly accounted for.

Riddiough (1997) considers an originator who needs to liquidate a share of his portfolio due to an external capital constraint, but faces adverse selection as he cannot credibly signal asset quality to the market. Riddiough shows that the creation of a riskless senior security (informationally insensitive) and the retention of the risky junior security (informationally sensitive) is the revenue maximizing strategy, as retaining[28] the FLP internalizes the lemon's related costs.[29] Pooling multiple assets is shown to be beneficial, as the likelihood of extreme outcomes can be reduced, which reduces the severity of the adverse selection problem. Furthermore, Riddiough allows debt renegotiation in case of borrower default and suggests to allocate control rights with the equity piece holder.[30] As just mentioned, Riddiough assumes that the originator is "newly capital constrained": an upper limit for the total investment value of the originator's portfolio drives the transaction. When considering CLOs, the motive thus is a regulatory one even though this is not explicitly stated and implemented rather generic, as risk characteristics of the different types of securities are not accounted for.

DeMarzo (2005) exploits the pooling and tranching of securities in different settings.[31] DeMarzo assumes that retaining a share of the assets to be securitized is a quality signal to uninformed investors. First, DeMarzo considers an informed agent who can either sell his assets individually or as a pool (pass-through structure). In this case, an information destruction effect results from pooling the assets: the decision on the share of assets retained is based on an

[28] Note that FLP retention is not a signaling device in Riddiough's model.

[29] In case the capital constraint is severe, a share of the junior security needs to be sold as well, and the originator incurs agency costs.

[30] The equity piece holder has better information on the underlying assets and, furthermore, is the first to be affected by losses in the underlying portfolio. However, ex post risk shifting incentives arise with equity piece holder control, which need to be addressed. See Riddiough (1997), p. 144.

[31] Major findings are based on DeMarzo / Duffie (1999).

average pool quality value only, the single asset information cannot be considered. Therefore, the informed agent would be better off selling the assets separately and thus making use of his private information. Subsequently, DeMarzo analyzes if pooling and tranching (pay-through structure) can be beneficial to informed agents. Pooling and tranching allows to construct a low risk security with greater liquidity and is therefore valuable. Pooling and tranching of assets will be preferred if these diversification benefits can be realized, and if these benefits exceed the information destruction effect mentioned above.[32] The analysis in DeMarzo (2005) is carried out from the perspective of the originator; his revenues are maximized. The transaction motive incorporated in DeMarzo (2005) is to raise funds for new investment opportunities. DeMarzo assumes the originator has access to investment opportunities with above market returns and, therefore, needs to free up capital to undertake these investments, with securitization being the only means to raise capital.[33]

Plantin (2004) addresses the adverse selection problem as well and models explicitly the sale of the first loss piece. Plantin considers a revenue maximizing investment bank facing different market participants who have different abilities in screening the collateral and in redistributing the securities. By assumption, good screeners have bad redistribution skills (e.g. hedge funds) and bad screeners have good redistribution skills (e.g. banks), and both need to distribute their investments, i.e. find an investor. Plantin analyzed different possible settings. In case information asymmetry on the underlying asset pool is low, it is profitable to create a junior security in order to attract sophisticated investors. In case information asymmetry on the underlying asset pool is high, a senior security needs to be created to protect unsophisticated investors from competing with sophisticated investors. Hence, in both cases a structure similar to that derived in Boot and Thakor is optimal. In case the number of market participants is augmented, the optimal number of tranches rises.

[32] DeMarzo also analyzes securitization from the perspective of an uninformed agent who faces informed and uninformed investors. Summing up the different scenarios above, DeMarzo develops a dynamic model of financial intermediation.

[33] Technically, DeMarzo assumes a higher internal discount rate for on balance sheet assets, see DeMarzo (2005), p. 7.

2.3.2 Ex post asymmetries and moral hazard

Gorton and Pennacchi (1995) focus on loan sales and analyze a setting where the value of bank loans depends on the bank's monitoring activities. In case a loan is sold to an external investor, the bank has no longer an incentive to exert effective monitoring.[34] Gorton and Pennacchi incorporate two structural elements to mitigate moral hazard: the retention of a share of the loan and the provision of a partial guarantee. The authors show that the share of the loan, which needs to be retained, is a function of the bank's internal funding costs, of the bank's default risk (as a proxy for the value of the guarantee), and of the riskiness of the loan. The share of a loan retained is the smaller, the greater the internal funding costs, the higher the quality of the loan, and the lower the bank's default probability. Gorton and Pennacchi take an originator's perspective and maximize his revenues from loan sales. Loan sales are driven by high internal funding cost, which can be interpreted as regulatory costs as well as economic costs.

The main objective of Gorton and Souleles (2005) is to analyze how asset securitization creates value. Gorton and Souleles do not incorporate a specific motive for asset securitization, their approach rather goes the opposite direction: given there is a certain amount of securitization, value drivers shall be identified. They focus on a bank which can fund two investment projects whose values are a function of the bank's unobservable effort choice. One of the projects can be financed off-balance sheet using an SPV (securitization). Furthermore, the bank enjoys a tax shield in case of on-balance sheet financing, but also faces bankruptcy costs. Results show that the value of securitization is increasing in the bankruptcy costs, decreasing in the tax rate, and increasing in the riskiness of the projects. Gorton and Souleles add a further agency conflict to their analysis: in that extension of their model, the bank can allocate projects on- or off-balance sheet after the project outcome is known to the bank but not to investors. Providing the bank with this additional option creates a lemons' problem; investors

[34] Instead of monitoring, one can also consider the bank's screening activity of potential borrowers before lending to them, which is the focus of Gorton / Pennacchi (1995). However, the model suits as well when considering the bank's activity as a monitoring effort. See Gorton / Pennacchi (1995), pp. 395-397.

are no longer willing to invest in the SPV. For that special setting, Gorton and Souleles show the existence of an equilibrium in an infinitely repeated game, making SPV financing viable and value creating, as bankruptcy costs can be avoided.

2.3.3 Implications and critical issues

The review above shows that FLP retention can serve to mitigate agency conflicts. Retaining the FLP can serve as signal when asset quality is uncertain ex ante. Equally, FLP retention can provide the originator with proper incentives in case of moral hazard. However, selling the FLP can also be explained with existing evidence. In Boot and Thakor (1993) and in Plantin (2004) selling the FLP is possible. Both articles suggest to partition cash flows in informationally sensitive and informationally insensitive tranches. Furthermore, both articles assume the existence of sophisticated investors who are able to purchase the informationally sensitive security, which is the FLP in the context of asset securitization. They thus focus on the demand side of the transaction when explaining the possibility to sell the FLP. Particularities concerning the FLP as well as varying transaction motives by the originator are not incorporated in their analysis.

The following analysis will show that selling the FLP in securitization transactions can be explained also without relying on the existence of sophisticated investors. Given the securitization of assets is value creating, originators might be inclined to maintain the ability to access this special market and optimize their activities according to a long-term horizon. The following section will formalize this way of thought. Furthermore, the articles reviewed above focus primarily on the *how*-component of securitization and not too much on the *why*-component. Motives for asset securitization are integrated rather scarce while the security design is analyzed in depth. Regulatory incentives would, for example, require a differentiated treatment of different types of securities, especially for Basel II. However, Basel II was not yet taken into account due to its non-existence during the formation period of most of the reviewed articles. Therefore, two transaction drivers will be considered in the following by first considering an originator who needs to raise funds and second an originator who faces a shortage of regulatory capital.

2.4 Two models on asset securitization

2.4.1 Model 1: Using CLOs to refinance growth opportunities

2.4.1.1 Model setup

In the following model the single driver of securitization is to raise funds for new investment projects.[35] There is a risk neutral originator O, for example a bank. O is endowed with initial wealth of C units in $t = 0$ and has exclusive access to a one-period investment opportunity C with a third party which requires an investment of C in $t = 0$.[36] Project C can be thought of as a credit or a portfolio of credits. The terms project C and credit C are used interchangeably in the following. Credit C is backed by an asset (or a portfolio of assets) that can take one out of two possible values in $t = 1$: asset value can either be high, F^H, or low, F^L. The repayment amount of credit C is fixed at an amount of $C(1+i)$ due at $t = 1$. In case asset value is high, payment obligations from credit C can fully be met by the obligor, in case asset value is low, payment obligations cannot fully be met, i.e. $F^H \geq C(1+i) > F^L$. F^L can hence be interpreted as a recovery value in case of default. Furthermore, the asset value is a function of the originator's monitoring activity e, with e being the probability of reaching the high asset value, and the low asset value being reached with opposite probability $(1-e)$. The originator can either engage in a high level of monitoring e_h, which leads to the asset value F^H with certainty (i.e. $e_h = 1$) and thus to a repayment of $C(1+i)$, or engage in a low level of monitoring e_l, with $0 < e_l < 1$, which leads to an expected repayment of $\mu(e_l) = e_l C(1+i) + (1-e_l)F^L$. The

[35] The setting chosen is similar to Gorton / Pennacchi (1995) and Riddiough (1997). Note that the moral hazard conflict highlighted here and the adverse selection problem are closely related. See Gorton / Pennacchi (1995), p. 397.

[36] The originator's initial endowment is not further specified in model 1 and could be either debt, equity, or both. Potential conflicts arising from the originator's capital structure (owner-manager conflicts, debt-holder equity-holder conflicts) are not taken account for. See Rudolph (2006), chapter 6 for an illustration of the relevant literature.

expected repayment of credit C is hence a function of the originator's monitoring level:

$$Repayment_C^{t=1} = \begin{cases} C(1+i) & \text{if } e = e_h \\ \mu(e_l) & \text{if } e = e_l \end{cases}$$

The monitoring activity induces costs of $c(e_h)$ and $c(e_l)$ respectively with $c(e_h) > c(e_l)$ at the originator. It is assumed that

$$C(1+i) - c(e_h) > \mu(e_l) - c(e_l) \tag{A.1}$$

and that

$$r_C = \frac{C(1+i) - c(e_h) - C}{C} > r_f \tag{A.2}$$

with r_C being the return of credit C and r_f $(r_f > 0)$ being the riskless rate of interest.[37] Hence, without further externalities, O will engage in credit C in $t = 0$, choose the high monitoring level e_h and realize a return of r_C. O can be considered being a financial intermediary with access to NPV positive investment projects that require monitoring in order to be successful.[38]

Immediately after $t = 0$ (in $t = 0^+$), an additional investment opportunity G arises to the originator (exclusively), as illustrated in figure 2.1. This opportunity can be thought of growth opportunities and carries an expected return of $\gamma > r_f$. Furthermore, project G requires no smallest investment unit and is not limited in size. As project G is assumed to be NPV positive, O is willing to carry it out. However, O has invested all available funds in credit C and therefore needs to raise additional funding. The only possibility to do so in this model is to sell the existing credit C to the market.[39]

Credit C can either be sold whole or cash flows can be structured before claims are sold to the market. While the whole sale corresponds to a pass-

[37] Note that assumption A.1 implies an upper bound on e_l: $e_l < (C(1+i) - F^L - c(e_h) + c(e_l))/(C(1+i) - F^L)$.

[38] The originator can be thought of being an intermediary as described by Diamond (1984) who however has some bargaining power and hence shares profits with entrepreneurs.

[39] As it is not the objective to evaluate securitization compared to other mechanisms of funding such as for example issuing equity this assumption seems justified.

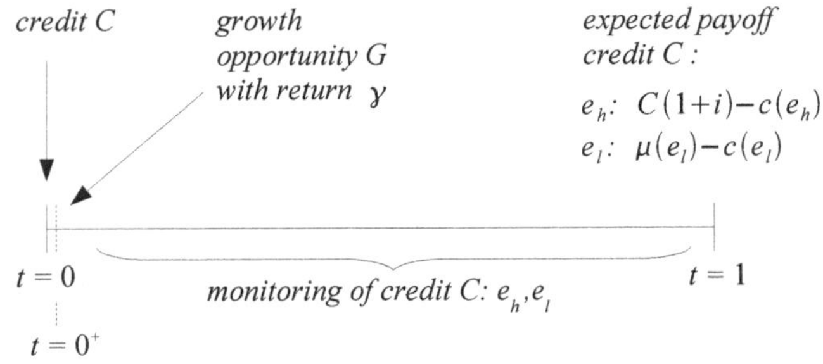

Figure 2.1: Time structure

through structure in terms of securitization it is referred to as whole sale in the following. The pay-through structure, hence when cash flows are structured before claims are sold to investors, is referred to as securitization in the following, but equally can be interpreted as a loan sale where only proportional claims to the cash flows of project C are sold. For both the 'whole sale' and 'securitization' it is assumed, that the newly created security is solely backed by the underlying asset. The potential investor has neither recourse to the originator nor a legal relationship with the debtor of credit C. This setting corresponds to the typical special purpose vehicle structure chosen in securitization transactions, where the no recourse clause is a legal building block. Moreover, regulatory capital relief can only be achieved by a loan seller, in this setting the originator, in case risks are effectively transferred, which is only given in case the risk taker's claim does solely rely on the cash flows of the underlying asset. Further, in this setting the originator remains the servicer of project C, and is the only one to provide value generating monitoring even in case credit C is sold to the market. Together, this setting corresponds very well to the observed structuring of CLOs.

On the buy-side, the market consists of a single risk neutral investor. The investor knows the distribution of *e* but is not able to observe the actual monitoring level chosen by O and is therefore exposed to moral hazard. Given this setting, the originator will try to find a structure that allows selling a share of credit C as large as possible without incurring agency costs in order to reinvest the proceeds in the growth opportunity G.

In the following section outcomes for the whole sale structure and for securitization are analyzed. Even though not common in securitization practice, it is also shortly lined out that the first-best solution could be achieved by contractually specifying a state-dependent fine to be borne by the originator. Section 2.4.1.3 extends the analysis to a long-term relationship of the investor and the originator by repeating the stage game, without relying on contractual features such as a fine.

2.4.1.2 Whole sale vs. securitization

As just lined out the originator will try to maximize the revenues from selling credit C to the investor. The negotiation process on the price and structure of the transaction is assumed to be as follows in the one-period setting: the originator will make an offer (take-it-or-leave-it), the investor can either accept or reject. In case the investor rejects, the originator will not be able to engage in project G and choose e_h. In case the investor accepts, the originator will invest the proceeds in project G and choose either e_h or e_l. It is assumed that full negotiation power is with the originator, however any bargaining game could be specified granting the investor bargaining power. The investor has an alternative investment technology yielding r_f and, as highlighted above, faces moral hazard. The originator thus has to find the security design that maximizes his payoff with respect to the constraint of granting a yield of at least r_f to the investor.

First it shall be analyzed which price can be attained in a whole sale of credit C (i.e. when selling a claim to all cash flows resulting from credit C). Assuming the investor believes that the originator will choose e_h, the maximum price the investor would be willing to pay would be $\delta C(1+i)$, with δ being the discount rate $\delta = 1/(1+r_f)$. However, as a default of credit C does no longer accrue at the originator in case of a whole sale, the originator has no incentive to choose e_h. With the investor anticipating the opportunistic behavior, the maximal price the investor is willing to pay for the whole credit C is $\delta\mu(e_l)$. Given this price the originator would still not engage in the high level of monitoring, as the expected gains $(C(1+i) - \mu(e_l))$ would accrue at the investor while the originator suffers the higher disutility from choosing e_h. Hence, the only feasible price is $\delta\mu(e_l)$, and will be offered by the originator if

$$(1+\gamma)\delta\mu(e_l)-c(e_l)\geq C(1+i)-c(e_h)\ .^{40} \tag{2.1}$$

As can be seen from assumption A.1 this will only be the case when γ, the return of project G, is sufficiently high. Also from A.1 it can be seen, that selling the asset whole at price $\delta C(1+i)$, committing to the high monitoring effort, and reinvesting the proceeds in project G would always be preferable. However, due to the moral hazard problem, this result cannot be achieved in a whole sale. The originator will therefore try to find a structure that reduces agency costs.[41] As proposed in several studies, a reduction in agency costs can be achieved by partitioning the cash flows in senior and subordinated securities, hence by the securitization solution. Here, a fully protected senior tranche can have the maximal size of F^L.[42] As a tranche of size F^L (a claim of F^L in $t=1$) does not carry default risk, the investor would accept a price of δF^L in $t=0$. Selling a claim of F^L leaves the originator with the subordinated claim (the first loss piece), whose value depends on the monitoring effort chosen by the originator. The expected value of the FLP is either $C(1+i)-F^L$ in case of e_h or $\mu(e_l)-F^L$ in case of e_l. Given this security design, it is always optimal for the originator to choose e_h and realize a payoff of

$$Payoff_{Sec}=(1+\gamma)\delta F^L+C(1+i)-F^L-c(e_h)\ .$$

As a first result, securitization is always preferable to not selling credit C at all. Whether or not securitization is preferable to a whole sale depends on the severity of the moral hazard problem. Comparing the payoffs in case of a whole

[40] Note that it is sufficient to compare $t=1$ payoffs as the $t=0$ investment of C is the same for any structuring choice.

[41] Given the whole sale is preferable to not selling credit C (inequality 2.1 holds), agency costs level at $(1+\gamma)\delta(C(1+i)-\mu(e_l))-c(e_h)+c(e_l)$.

[42] Note that even with universal risk neutrality, the size of the senior tranche cannot be $\mu(e_l)$ as $\mu(e_l)$ is based on the upside potential of the underlying credit C. If however, the upside potential would be absorbed in the senior claim, a subordinated claim could not exist.

sale and in case of securitization with a senior security of size F^L shows that securitization is preferable in case

$$(1-(1+\gamma)\delta e_l)(C(1+i)-F^L) > c(e_h)-c(e_l) \ . \tag{2.2}$$

The left hand side of equation (2.2) is the expected increase of payoffs under securitization over the whole sale payoff, the right hand side displays the associated costs. With securitization and the choice of e_h, the value of the FLP can fully be realized in $t = 1$. With a whole sale, the increment $C(1+i)-F^L$ is realized with probability e_l and accounted for in the price of $\delta\mu(e_l)$ at $t = 0$, which allows a larger investment towards project G. A high level of γ hence supports the whole sale structure. Also, a whole sale is the preferable choice when the moral hazard problem is low. This is the case when e_l is high and hence, even though only the low amount of monitoring is chosen, the bad outcome is realized with a small probability. Contrary, benefits with securitization compared to a whole sale are especially high, when e_l is low and the moral hazard conflict therefore severe. Given the moral hazard conflict is severe the attractiveness of securitization rises in the size of the FLP (the lower the level of F^L).[43] Furthermore, securitization can only be preferable when costs associated with choosing e_h are not prohibitively high.

Given the severity of the agency conflict the appropriate structure for the transaction can be chosen by the originator. However, for both the whole sale as well as securitization agency costs remain. The originator would be better off in case he was able to credibly commit to choosing e_h and hence being able to collect a price of $\delta C(1+i)$ in $t = 0$. This would allow the maximal investment towards project G without incurring agency cost. This first-best outcome can be realized with two different solutions. First, a state-dependent fine can be imposed on the originator, which will be lined out shortly in the following. Second, without relying on a fine, there might exist pareto superior equilibria to those lined out above given long-term relationships among market participants, which will be lined out in the next section.

[43] Formally at least $e_l < 1/(1+\gamma)\delta$ has to hold to make this statement.

As highlighted above, the price $\delta C(1+i)$ for the whole sale cannot be achieved in a one-period game due to the moral hazard conflict. However, given the setting chosen here, an investor can verify the originator's monitoring level ex post in case of the bad state outcome, as the choice of e_h leads to an asset value of F^H with certainty. By imposing a fine on O in case the bad state outcome is realized, it is possible to incentivize O to choose e_h. Given the whole sale price of $\delta C(1+i)$ for asset C, the fine has to exceed a minimum threshold such that the expected payoff from choosing e_h exceeds the expected payoff from choosing e_l, given the fine is due in case the bad state outcome F^L is realized. The minimum threshold for the fine levels at $(c(e_h)-c(e_l))/(1-e_l)$ and is, due to assumption A.1, always met for a fine of $C(1+i)-F^L$.[44] The fine of $C(1+i)-F^L$ would exactly compensate the loss of the investor in case he paid the full price $\delta C(1+i)$ in $t=0$ but only the bad state outcome is realized. However, depending on the parameter constellations, a lower fine can be sufficient to appropriately incentivize the originator.

While a contractual feature like a fine can provide a solution in case the transaction is driven by funding requirements, such features are not common in securitization given the SPV structure and the no recourse clauses. Therefore, another mechanism is lined out in the following section that does not rely on a fine but on the repeated interaction of market participants.

2.4.1.3 Repeated securitization

Markets for asset securitization became more mature in the last decade with several market participants acting regularly on the market. Such a situation is well described by repeating the stage game analyzed above. In order to facilitate the following analysis it is assumed that equation (2.2) holds (securitization is preferable to a whole sale), and that the amount of capital available to the originator at the beginning of every period levels at C.[45]

---

44 The threshold results from $\delta C(1+i)(1+\gamma)-c(e_h) > e_l[\delta C(1+i)(1+\gamma)]+(1-e_l)[\delta C(1+i)(1+\gamma)-\text{fine}]-c(e_l)$.

45 Profits are hence disbursed at the end of every period, losses are compensated by the firm owners. Apparently this precludes an in depth analysis of the dynamics related to the capital structure of the originator. However, such questions are beyond the scope of this analysis.

As a starting point, the stage game analyzed above is reformulated more precisely in the following. Let the stage game be a dynamic game, with the investor moving first, the originator moving second. The investor has to decide upon two different take-it-or-leave-it offers: (i) he can either purchase a claim to all cash flows of credit C at the price $\delta C(1+i)$, or (ii) he can buy the senior tranche specified in section 2.4.1.2 above. The originator can thereafter decide upon choosing e_h or e_l. As already lined out, the originator has an incentive to shirk in case the investor would choose to agree to offer (i). The subgame-perfect outcome is [(ii); e_l, e_h] with the equilibrium path being [(ii), e_h].[46] However, if the originator was able to commit to e_h, a pareto superior outcome could be realized in case the investor would agree to the offer (i). The originator would benefit from a higher investment towards project G in $t=0$ and increase the $t=1$ payoff by $((1+\gamma)\delta-1)(C(1+i)-F^L)$, the investor would still realize the return r_f, now on a larger investment of $\delta C(1+i)$.[47] Such an equilibrium can possibly be supported in a repeated game. In case players interact repeatedly deviations from the equilibrium path can be punished in future periods. In case future punishments represent a reasonable threat to the players, players can be induced to play long-term efficient outcomes in each period. Such equilibria can be based on trigger strategies: players play long-term efficient strategies as long as no deviation from those strategies is detected. In case deviation is detected, a punishment period follows, thereafter players return to the long-term efficient outcome. The horizon for repeated games can be finitely or infinitely. In case no terminal date can be commonly foreseen in a repeated game the time horizon is set infinitely, which shall be the case here.[48] Reconsidering the stage game in an infinitely repeated context, one can verify if the equilibrium path [(i); e_h] can be supported in the repeated game given a specific punishment strategy.

---

[46] The expression [(ii); e_l, e_h] reads as follows: the first entry is the investor's strategy, the second entry is the originator's strategy. The originator's strategy displays the originator's reactions towards the investor's choices (i) and (ii), hence the originator chooses e_l off the equilibrium path and e_h being on the equilibrium path.

[47] This would not change the investor's overall position as he has access to an alternative investment technology yielding r_f as well.

[48] See Fudenberg / Tirole (1991), p. 147.

However, the analysis can also be slightly generalized: the situation faced by the investor is being the principal in a repeated moral hazard setting. An incentive compatible price has to be found that encourages the originator (the agent) to choose the high effort level, when a claim to all cash flows of credit C is sold.[49] Hence a minimum price P_{min} for the package of the junior and senior security has to be found that is sufficient to induce the monitoring level of e_h on the equilibrium path, given a punishment in a trigger strategy. This price P will in the following be proposed by the investor and needs to be accepted by the originator. The punishment is assumed to be the investor offering to purchase only the senior security at a price of δF^L, which will be accepted by the originator and lead to the choice of e_h. The punishment is hence equivalent to the one-period subgame-perfect equilibrium highlighted above.[50]

Taking this more general approach is appropriate, as no assumption regarding the negotiation power of the originator and the investor needs to be made ex ante. Furthermore, in case there exists a gap between the minimum incentive compatible price and the maximum price the investor is willing to pay, discounts to the price of the FLP, which exist according to anecdotic evidence, can be explained.

In order to define the strategies of the investor and the originator in this more general setting, consider a history as a *good* history when the price offered for the whole claim was some specific $P^* \geq P_{min}$, the price was always accepted by the originator and the outcome was always high. A history is *bad* otherwise. Note that history includes the current period which is important when analyzing the originator's behavior. The investor's strategy is to offer the price P^* for a claim to all cash flows of credit C in the first period and in every subsequent period in case history is good and to offer a price of δF^L for the senior security

[49] The methodological approach chosen for the analysis is closely related to the one used by Shapiro / Stiglitz (1984). See also Gibbons (1992), pp. 107-112 for a review. In case the high monitoring effort would not induce the high asset value with certainty, as it is the case in this model, an equilibrium in review strategies could be established. In review strategies the principal reviews the output periodically and, in case aggregated output falls below a threshold, changes to a punishment phase. Otherwise a new review phase begins. See Radner (1985).

[50] Another possible punishment would be the investor retreating from the market. As such a punishment is more severe, an equilibrium could be established more easily.

described above once history turned bad. The originator's strategy is to accept to sell a claim to all cash flows of credit C as long as $P > (C(1+i) - c(e_h) + c(e_l))/(1+\gamma)$—a threshold to be explained below—and to choose e_h in case the history of the play is good (including the current period), e_l otherwise. The originator rejects the offer for a claim to all cash flows of credit C in case $P < (C(1+i) - c(e_h) + c(e_l))/(1+\gamma)$ and chooses e_h. The originator accepts the offer of δF^L for the senior security and chooses e_h. The investor's strategy hence is a typical trigger strategy with an infinite punishment once deviation occurred. The originator's strategy is a trigger strategy as well, however slightly different, as the originator can react to deviations from the equilibrium path within the same period in this sequential game, which is why the threshold above needs to be accounted for in the originator's strategy. Particularly, the originator will optimize myopically given a deviation by the investor, as the punishment will be played forever thereafter.

In order to proof that these strategies form a subgame-perfect Nash equilibrium it must be shown that the strategies form a Nash equilibrium in every subgame. In an infinitely repeated game, every subgame is identical to the game as a whole. Here, subgames can be grouped in two categories: those beginning after a good history and those beginning after a bad history. In the following a subgame perfect equilibrium for the repeated game is developed.

Given a minimum price P_{min} can be found, two further steps are needed to establish a subgame-perfect equilibrium. First, it has to be shown that the price will be acceptable for the investor. Second, it has to be verified what happens outside the equilibrium path.

To begin with, the minimum incentive compatible price will be derived. Given price P for a claim to all cash flows of credit C and the choice of e_h by O, the firm value in $t = 1$ to O will be:

$$V_{e_h} = (1+\gamma)P - c(e_h) + \delta V_{e_h} \text{ .}^{51} \tag{2.3}$$

[51] Again it is sufficient to compare $t = 1$ payoffs as the $t = 0$ investment of C is identical across the different effort choices. Further, payoffs could equally be discounted to $t = 0$.

In case the originator chooses e_l deviation will be detected with probability $(1-e_l)$ which triggers punishment. Here, for simplicity, infinite punishment is assumed, which results in the following firm value:

$$V_{e_l} = (1+\gamma)P - c(e_l) + e_l \delta V_{e_l} + (1-e_l)\frac{\delta}{1-\delta} S \ , \tag{2.4}$$

where S is the payoff in case of securitizing the senior tranche F^L with

$$S \equiv (1+\gamma)\delta F^L + C(1+i) - F^L - c(e_h) \ .$$

The originator will hence be induced to choose e_h when offered P for a claim to all cash flows of credit C in case $V_{e_h} > V_{e_l}$, which yields a minimum incentive compatible price P_{min} of

$$P_{min} > \frac{S}{1+\gamma} + \frac{c(e_h)}{1+\gamma} + (c(e_h) - c(e_l))\frac{1-\delta}{\delta(1+\gamma)(1-e_l)} \ . \tag{2.5}$$

Note that the minimum price (reinvested at $(1+\gamma)$) exceeds the sum of the punishment payoff S and the cost associated with high effort $c(e_h)$, a premium must be paid to induce the optimal effort level.

Given price P satisfies equation (2.5) O will be induced to choose e_h. The next step is to verify that the price is acceptable to the investor. The investor will only propose a price $P > P_{min}$ in case his return on that price is at least r_f. The investor will therefore accept such a security design when

$$\frac{C(1+i) - P_{max}}{P_{max}} \geq r_f \ , \tag{2.6}$$

which is equivalent to $P_{max} \leq \delta C(1+i)$. Thus, for the existence of an equilibrium there has to be at least a δ for which $P_{min} < P_{max}$ holds. A lower bound δ^* for δ is derived in appendix A, hence with δ close enough to unity ($\delta > \delta^*$) a Nash equilibrium in the repeated game can be supported that allows to sell even the FLP at an appropriate price as the moral hazard conflict can be overcome. The price for the claim to all cash flows is subject to the bargaining power of the originator and the investor and has to lie somewhere between P_{min} and P_{max}. When all bargaining power is with the originator, the price will level at $\delta C(1+i)$, which sets the investor's return to r_f and maximizes the originator's payoff. When all bargaining power is with the investor, the price will level at P_{min}, the originator hence sells the claim to all cash flows at a discount and the investor realizes a return above the riskless rate.

In order to establish subgame-perfection it remains to show that the players' strategies form an equilibrium in every subgame. As mentioned above, subgames can be grouped in those beginning after a good history and in those beginning after a bad history. Given a good history it was shown above that with δ sufficiently large the players' strategies form a Nash equilibrium. It remains to verify that the players' strategies form a Nash equilibrium given a bad history. When history is bad the originator will always choose e_l in case a claim to all cash flows of credit C is sold, therefore the investor will only offer to buy the senior security at price δF^L. Considering the originator, in case history is bad the investor will offer only to purchase the senior security in the subsequent period and thereafter, so that the originator should optimize the one-period action. He should accept in case the payoff from accepting the offer for the whole claim and shirking exceeds the maximum payoff without securitization ($(1+\gamma)P - c(e_l) > C(1+i) - c(e_h)$) and in that case choose e_l, reject otherwise and choose e_h. This corresponds exactly to the players' strategies, therefore a subgame-perfect equilibrium to the repeated game exists.

Interestingly, the minimum incentive compatible price for the FLP on a stand-alone basis can be easily obtained from the analysis above. By substituting $\delta F^L + P_{FLP}$ for P in equation (2.3) and (2.4) it can be seen that P_{FLP} at least has to level at $P_{min} - \delta F^L$ to be incentive compatible. Therefore, the FLP and the senior security can also be sold separately, with the discount—in case bargaining power is with the investor—only applying to the FLP. The FLP thus is priced in the range of $P_{min} - \delta F^L$ and $\delta(C(1+i) - F^L)$, given δ being close enough to unity. The senior security is always priced at δF^L. The game specified above for a claim to all cash flows of credit C could thus be specified for the FLP only. The investor's punishment strategy would be to retreat from the market for first loss pieces in case of default.

Summarizing the results from model 1, several insights can be gained. In a one-period setting the choice of a whole sale structure or securitization depends on the severity of the agency conflict. In case the moral hazard conflict is severe, it is optimal to only sell a riskless senior security and retain the FLP as the agency conflict can be mitigated. However, FLP retention comes at a cost: by retaining a share of the asset, the amount to be reinvested in the growth opportunity G is below the reinvestment amount for the whole sale structure. A fine to be borne by the originator can impose the first-best solution in the one-period game, but is not typical for securitization structures. Considering a repeated game, it is shown that the FLP can be sold at an appropriate price while the incentives for the originator to monitor the underlying asset are maintained without relying on a fine. Hence the reinvestment towards project G is maximized while still solving the agency conflict. A discount to the price of the FLP can apply and is subject to the bargaining power of the originator and the investor.

2.4.2 Model 2: Using CLOs to manage regulatory capital

2.4.2.1 Changes to the model setup

Other than model 1 presented above, the following model focuses on regulatory risk transfer. The risk neutral originator is subject to prudent regulation that fully protects debt capital providers (depositors). While the general game structure remains unchanged compared to model 1, several details are subject to changes and some further assumptions become necessary. Doing so, the attempt is not to integrate the regulatory framework in every detail but to develop a stylized model that illustrates the major implications for asset securitization due to regulation. Different approaches within Basel II are therefore not differentiated in the following, furthermore, as noted above, the actually proposed changes to the new regulatory framework are neither taken into account.

The basic approach for calculating regulatory capital requirements for any asset is the same for Basel I as well as for Basel II, but differs in its parametrization. Capital requirements are derived by multiplying the exposure at default

(EAD) of the relevant asset with the corresponding risk weighting and the minimum capital ratio of 8%. In this model, for Basel I and for Basel II, the exposure at default corresponds to the book value of the relevant project, with the book value being the project's notional amount C.[52] The regulator has the same access to information as the investor and is assumed to define risk weighting factors such that regulatory capital is sufficient to absorb all possible losses that can arise from a financial claim.[53] Whether the risk is associated to the underlying asset itself or to the originator's behavior is not of the regulator's concern, the regulator only focuses on the possible default event and full protection of depositors.[54] Hence, differences between Basel I and Basel II only concern the risk weighting factors in this model as the EAD is constant at C.

Under the Basel I regime, the risk weighting factors for project C and G, rw_C and rw_G, only depend on the *debtor category* and therefore are constants, denoted as rw_C^{BI} and rw_G^{BI}. Given a debtor category specific lower bound for the asset value of projects belonging to that specific category, the risk weighting must be such that the maximum loss can be absorbed. Define $\underline{F^L}$ as the relevant category specific lower bound for project C, the risk weighting for project C

[52] Setting the exposure at default equal to the notional amount of a project includes an assumption concerning the effective accounting standard, as book values vary across accounting standards. Under German law, to take an example, a newly created claim is accounted for with the costs of its acquisition, see § 340e HGB and § 253 HGB. These costs correspond, in this model, to the notional amount as there is no premium or discount. The model thus fits well to German accounting standards. When considering IAS 39, the book value of a newly created claim is its fair value including transaction costs. One could assume the originator setting the fair value of credit C at C by discounting future payoffs of $C(1+i)$ with i at $t=0$. Given this assumption and the fact that there are no transaction costs in this model, the model also fits quite well to international accounting standards.
Furthermore, note that the EAD is specified differently across the different regulatory approaches. However, as no specific provisions or partial write-offs occur in this model these differences need not be accounted for.

[53] This clearly is not an exact model of the regulatory framework, however sufficient to capture the mechanics of regulation. IRB approaches are, to take an example, based on a value at risk approach and do capture losses at a confidence level of 99.9%. See Hofmann / Pluto (2005) for central aspects of Basel II. Here, in the (non-granular) one asset case, regulation can be tailored explicitly to the possible default event.

[54] For further insights on the economics of bank regulation see Bhattacharya / Boot / Thakor (1998) and Dewatripont / Tirole (1994).

must be such that $C - \underline{F}^L = C \cdot rw_C^{BI} \cdot 8\%$ holds, hence

$$rw_C^{BI} = \frac{C - \underline{F}^L}{C \cdot 8\%} \ .$$

Under Basel II, risk weightings are asset specific. The risk weighting for project C is a function of F^L and again specified such that the maximum loss from project C can be absorbed by the equity capital, hence

$$rw_C^{BII} = \frac{C - F^L}{C \cdot 8\%} \ .$$

To exclude the possibility of negative regulatory capital requirements it is assumed that $C > F^L$, which implies that $C > \underline{F}^L$ holds as well.

Concerning the growth opportunity G, the risk weighting factors are not explicitly specified. As noted above, rw_G^{BI} is a constant and equals rw_C^{BI} in case project G is from the same debtor category as project C. Under the Basel II regime, rw_G^{BII} is risk sensitive. Given that risk increases with the expected return, one can define rw_G^{BII} as a function of γ, with $\partial rw_G^{BII}(\gamma)/\partial\gamma > 0$.

Turning back to the analysis of the model, the parties involved in the model and the game structure laid out in section 2.4.1.1 remains unchanged. Hence, the originator O has access to project C in $t = 0$, and the project's performance is subject to the originator's monitoring effort. Furthermore, just as in model 1, the growth opportunity G arises in $t = 0^+$. Also, risk neutrality is still assumed for both the originator and the investor.[55] Opposed to model 1, the scarce resource now is regulatory capital. It is assumed that the originator's available equity capital levels at $C \cdot rw_C \cdot 8\%$ and hence matches perfectly with the necessary regulatory capital to engage in project C. The originator is not able to alter the amount of equity capital in the short run, however, other than in model 1, the originator is able to raise external debt financing (e.g. by depositors) in this

[55] Note that the model does not crucially depend on the degree of risk aversion of the originator and the investor. Concerning the regulatory context of this section, where depositors need to be protected by prudent regulators, one could argue that investors should be risk averse. This would imply a discount to the whole sale price due to the uncertainty of the associated cash flows and thus make securitization more favorable. General results of the model would however remain unchanged. In general, risk aversion would play a more prominent role when the focus was set not only on tranching but also on pooling.

model.[56] Due to the regulatory framework, debt capital is perfectly protected and thus available at the risk free rate r_f, investments at r_f are possible as well. As credit C is an NPV positive investment opportunity for the originator he will take up the necessary amount of debt $C - C \cdot rw_C \cdot 8\%$ and pursue project C in $t = 0$. The originator is hence a stylized bank that fully leverages the available regulatory capital. Activities are financed by debt, e.g. deposits, and equity with debt capital being fully protected.

Project C ties up all available regulatory capital. Consequently, an investment towards the growth opportunity G in $t = 0^+$ is only possible when either regulatory capital is freed up or additional capital is raised. By assumption the originator is not able to raise additional equity or equity-like capital externally in $t = 0^+$, so that freeing up regulatory capital is the only means of pursuing the growth opportunity. The originator can do so by selling or securitizing credit C. Even though the originator is not able to alter the amount of equity capital exogenously, the amount of available regulatory capital can change endogenously as realized gains from selling credit C increase (respectively losses decrease) equity capital.

The subsequent analysis focuses on the implications for security design given the shortage of regulatory capital and an NPV positive growth opportunity. The old and the new regulatory framework will be considered. The prevailing agency conflict and its remedy is equivalent to model 1 above, but implications for the overall payoff differ due to the regulatory transaction motive. Other than in model 1, equity payoffs are compared opposed to overall payoffs, as the originator is now considered being an owner-manager who provides equity capital. However, as debt capital is riskless the overall payoff could be considered as well as risk shifting is not possible in this setting.

2.4.2.2 Whole sale vs. securitization under the Basel I regime

In the regulatory context as well, there are two possibilities for the security design, whole sale or securitization. A contractual design based on a state depen-

[56] As changes to the level of equity commonly require the approval of the shareholders' meeting the assumption of a fixed level of equity capital in the short term seems reasonable.

dent fine is not considered in the following, as such a fine implies risk retention by the originator, and risk transfer is not approved by the regulatory entities for such a structure.

When choosing a whole sale structure, the originator can achieve a price of $\delta\mu(e_l)$ due to moral hazard, just like in model 1. With regulatory capital being the scarce resource, the impact of a whole sale (at $t = 0^+$) of project C on regulatory capital has to be proven. There are two effects which need to be taken into account. First, the amount of assets removed from the balance sheet has to be considered. Second, as gains increase and losses decrease equity and hence regulatory capital, it is to analyze whether the whole sale is profitable or not. In a whole sale structure, project C is removed entirely from the balance sheet, profits or losses of a whole sale depend on the parameter values. When structuring a whole sale the originator will choose the low effort level as benefits accrue only at the investor, hence the profit from a whole sale can be written as

$$profit_{WS} = \delta\mu(e_l) - \delta c(e_l) - C \ ,$$

where it is assumed that the costs related to the project occur at the end of the period and are hence discounted.[57] As $C(1+i) > \mu(e_l) > F^L$ holds the profit can be either positive or negative. Adding the profit to the regulatory capital that was available in $t = 0$ results in the $t = 0^+$ regulatory capital (*reg cap*)

$$reg\ cap_{WS}^{t=0^+} = C \cdot rw_C^{BI} \cdot 8\% + (\delta\mu(e_l) - \delta c(e_l) - C) = \delta(\mu(e_l) - c(e_l)) - \underline{F^L}$$

which determines the extent to which the growth opportunity G can be pursued. The feasible exposure G_{WS}^{BI} towards project G can be derived by setting the required regulatory capital for project G equal to the available regulatory capital and levels at

$$G_{WS}^{BI} = \frac{reg\ cap_{WS}^{t=0^+}}{rw_G^{BI} \cdot 8\%} = \frac{\delta(\mu(e_l) - c(e_l)) - \underline{F^L}}{rw_G^{BI} \cdot 8\%} \ .$$

[57] As the project is sold entirely costs are assigned in $t = 0$.

The proceeds from the whole sale are used to fund project G, where either excess returns are invested at r_f or, in case a funding gap remains, debt is raised at the cost of r_f. The originator's decision whether to choose a whole sale or not depends on the overall return on the $t=0$ equity investment and hence on the $t=1$ equity payoff. The end of period payoff consists of the return on project G and the compounded whole sale payoff less funding expenses and monitoring costs, and can be written as[58]

$$equity\,{}_{WS}^{t=1} = G_{WS}^{BI}(\gamma - r_f) + \mu(e_l) - c(e_l) - \underline{F}^L(1+r_f) \quad . \tag{2.7}$$

Of course the originator could also not sell project C, which results in an equity payoff of $C(1+i) - c(e_h) - \underline{F}^L(1+r_f)$. Equivalent to model 1, due to assumption A.1, a whole sale is only preferable to not selling project C when γ is sufficiently large.

Alternatively, the originator can choose to securitize project C in the same way as in model 1, by selling a senior security of size F^L (a claim of F^L at $t=1$) at a price of δF^L. Again, the impact of the transaction on regulatory capital has to be analyzed. In the case of securitization, assets are not entirely removed from the balance sheet when the FLP is retained, the junior security of size $C - F^L$ (notional) needs to be fully deducted from the available regulatory capital. Other than for the whole sale structure, securitization does not result in profits or losses in $t=0^+$. A claim of size F^L in $t=1$, worth δF^L in $t=0^+$, is sold at a price of δF^L. Profits are achieved with the retained FLP and are realized in $t=1$, therefore the costs of $c(e_h)$ are assigned to $t=1$. The $t=0^+$ available regulatory capital hence levels at

$$reg\ cap\,{}_{Sec}^{t=0^+} = C \cdot rw_C^{BI} \cdot 8\% - (C - F^L)$$

and allows an investment towards project G of

$$G_{Sec}^{BI} = \frac{reg\ cap\,{}_{Sec}^{t=0^+}}{rw_G^{BI} \cdot 8\%} = \frac{F^L - \underline{F}^L}{rw_G^{BI} \cdot 8\%} \quad .$$

[58] In extensive form: $equity\,{}_{WS}^{t=1} = G_{WS}^{BI}(1+\gamma) - (G_{WS}^{BI} - \delta\mu(e_l))(1+r_f) - c(e_l) - \underline{F}^L(1+r_f)$.

Equivalent to the whole sale structure, the proceeds from selling the senior security are used to finance project G, additional funds can be raised at r_f if necessary. Opposed to the whole sale structure, the originator is induced to choose the high effort level e_h and is hence able to avoid agency costs. The overall equity payoff in $t=1$ when choosing the securitization structure results in

$$equity_{Sec}^{t=1} = G_{Sec}^{BI}(\gamma - r_f) + C(1+i) - c(e_h) - \underline{F}^L(1+r_f) \ . \qquad (2.8)$$

From equation (2.8) it can be seen that securitization is always at least as good as not selling project C at all.

For both the whole sale and securitization, the payoff is the higher, the less severe the bad state outcome, i.e. the higher F^L. For the whole sale, a higher level of F^L increases both the whole sale price as well as the available regulatory capital, in the securitization structure only the available regulatory capital is affected and also increases with increasing F^L. In case F^L corresponds to the lower bound $\underline{F}^L$ securitization cannot free up regulatory capital, whereas a whole sale structure can in case e_l is high. Also for both the whole sale and securitization, the payoff is the higher, the higher the return on project G given the constant risk weighting factor.

Comparing the payoffs from a whole sale and securitization, results are similar to those of model 1 above. A whole sale is only the preferable solution in case the moral hazard conflict is weak, i.e. when e_l takes a high value. Otherwise, securitization is the preferable choice.

More generally, the model describes very well the incentives provided by the Basel I regime, namely to sell high quality assets and to engage in low quality asset. Selling project C is the more attractive the higher the difference $F^L - \underline{F}^L$, i.e. the higher the asset quality. The reinvestment towards project G is the more attractive, the higher the expected return γ and hence the riskier the growth opportunity given a constant risk weighting factor.[59] In the following section

[59] Of course the return of project G is not entirely independent of the risk weighting, as for G as well it is assumed that all potential losses can be absorbed by the regulatory capital.

it can be seen that theses distorting incentives were mitigated under the new regulatory framework.

2.4.2.3 Whole sale vs. securitization under the Basel II regime

Turning to the new regulatory framework Basel II, results change as the risk sensitive weighting factors need to be considered. In order to allow some comparison to the Basel I setting, the same absolute amount of ($t = 0$) available regulatory capital is considered here, hence $C - \underline{F^L}$. Due to the objective of modeling the shortage of regulatory capital as sole transaction driver, it must be assumed that the asset quality of project C is at the lower bound $\underline{F^L}$ so that the available regulatory capital matches perfectly with the required amount of regulatory capital.[60]

The payoffs for a whole sale structure as well as for securitization in $t = 1$ can be derived the same way as in the Basel I setting above. Defining the expected credit value given the low monitoring level e_l as $\underline{\mu(e_l)} = e_l C(1+i) + (1-e_l)\underline{F^L}$, the feasible exposure in $t = 0^+$ towards project G when choosing a whole sale levels at

$$G_{WS}^{BII} = \frac{reg\ cap\ {}_{WS}^{t=0^+}}{rw_G^{BII} \cdot 8\%} = \frac{\delta(\underline{\mu(e_l)} - c(e_l)) - \underline{F^L}}{rw_G^{BII} \cdot 8\%} ,$$

which results in the $t = 1$ equity payoff of

$$equity\ {}_{WS}^{t=1} = G_{WS}^{BII}(\gamma - r_f) + \underline{\mu(e_l)} - c(e_l) - \underline{F^L}(1 + r_f) \ . \tag{2.9}$$

Comparing equation (2.9) to equation (2.7) highlights the main change in the new regulatory setting. Reconsidering the Basel I setting, equation (2.7) equals equation (2.9) when F^L equals $\underline{F^L}$. Given the quality of project C is above the lower bound ($F^L > \underline{F^L}$), the whole sale equity payoff in $t = 1$ rises in

---

60 Alternatively, the model could be specified such that the quality of project C can take any value F^L. The shortage of regulatory capital would then be integrated by setting the $t = 0$ available regulatory capital to $C - F^L$. However, this implies varying absolute levels of ex ante available regulatory capital, which would lead to a low level of comparability of payoffs for the old and the new regulatory regime and raise difficulties when considering comparative statics for the Basel II regime.

the Basel I setting (equation (2.7)) as the $t = 0^+$ available regulatory capital as well as the whole sale price grows in F^L. These incentives to sell high quality assets no longer exist with the new regulatory framework as a higher level of F^L implies a lower level of ex ante required regulatory capital (namely $C - F^L$) for project C. The higher the asset quality, the less severe to need to free up regulatory capital, as there is still regulatory capital available ($F^L - \underline{F^L}$) for the growth opportunity. Given project C's quality is at the lower bound $\underline{F^L}$ and γ is sufficiently high, the equity payoff from a whole sale in the Basel II regime exceeds the payoff from not selling project C only in case the moral hazard conflict is low (e_l is sufficiently high). Again, a higher level of γ increases the $t = 1$ whole sale payoff. However, as the risk weighting factor is risk sensitive now, a higher expected return for project G results in a lower feasible exposure towards the project. Given risk weightings are calibrated properly, the increases in expected payoffs should be offset by a reduction in the feasible exposure.

Turning to securitization and again given the shortage of regulatory capital under the Basel II regime, it is not possible to free up regulatory capital when the FLP is retained in this model. Since the regulatory capital matches perfectly the size of the FLP, and the FLP needs to be deducted from regulatory capital when retained, the $t = 0^+$ available regulatory capital is zero. The payoff from securitization therefore equals the payoff from not selling project C at all, as no additional revenue from project G can be generated but the high effort level is still induced and the high project value thus realized through the value of the FLP and the reinvestment of the proceeds from the senior security. For higher levels of F^L, it would be neither possible to free up regulatory capital. However, here as well, the ex ante required amount of regulatory capital would be lower which would reduce the need to free regulatory capital ex ante.

Comparing the whole sale and securitization given regulatory capital is scarce, only a whole sale can set free regulatory capital given the moral hazard conflict is low. Contrary, given a severe moral hazard conflict, it is not possible to free regulatory capital neither in a whole sale nor in securitization in case the FLP needs to be retained. Selling the FLP however would result in a complete relief of regulatory capital and allow a significant investment towards the growth opportunity. The ability to sell the FLP is hence of significant importance under the Basel II regime. In the following it will be shown that, for the regulatory setting as well, selling the FLP is possible in a repeated game setting. Due to the high importance of this matter for the new regulatory regime, the repeated game will be analyzed for the Basel II setting. The game is set up in analogy to the repeated game analyzed for the case of refinancing needs. The following section therefore only lines out the structure of the game and gives an outline of out how to establish the subgame-perfect equilibrium. All details are presented in appendix B.

2.4.2.4 Repeated securitization under the Basel II regime

In this section an equilibrium in a repeated game setting is derived for the new regulatory framework. It is assumed that the moral hazard conflict is severe (e_l is sufficiently low), so that the whole sale yields a lower payoff than not selling project C in the one-period game. Hence, the originator is indifferent towards choosing not to sell project C or to securitize the senior security, as both strategies yield the same payoff.

Again, a pareto superior result could be achieved in case the FLP could be sold, i.e. in case the investor would purchase a claim to all cash flows of project C at a reasonable price. The originator would benefit from a release of regulatory capital allowing an investment towards project G, the investor, depending on the bargaining situation, realizes either the return r_f or more. Assuming that market participants interact repeatedly, the one-period game is now analyzed in an infinitely repeated game context, where again—analog to section 2.4.1.3—the focus is set on the generalized framework: an incentive compatible price for a claim to all cash flows of project C is derived that induces the originator to exert the high effort given a punishment by the investor. Now, the punishment is assumed to be the investor retreating from the market entirely. Alternatively, buying only the senior security could be specified as punishment strategy with the resulting payoff to the originator being the same. Punishment again is played forever once deviation was detected. The punishment results in a choice of e_h by the originator and is the subgame-perfect outcome of the game analyzed in section 2.4.2.3 given the assumption that the moral hazard conflict is severe. Furthermore, the amount of equity capital in the beginning of every period levels at $C - \underline{F^L}$.[61]

Analog to model 1, a history is a *good* history in case the price offered by the investor for the claim to all cash flows was some specific $P^{**} \geq P_{min}$, the price was always accepted by the originator and the outcome was always high. A history is a *bad* history otherwise. Again, history includes the current period. This allows to define the players' strategies, with the investor offering the price P^{**} for a claim to all cash flows of credit C in the first period and in every subsequent period in case history was good and not to make an offer once history turned bad. The originator's strategy is to accept to sell a claim to all cash flows of project C in case $P > \tilde{P}$—the threshold $\tilde{P}$ is derived in appendix B.1—and to choose e_h in case history is good, e_l otherwise. The originator rejects the offer for a claim to all cash flows of credit C in case $P < \tilde{P}$ and chooses e_h. The originator chooses e_h in case the investor does not offer to buy any claims to the cash flows of project C.

Again, it must be verified that these strategies form an equilibrium in every subgame in order to establish a subgame-perfect Nash equilibrium. Considering the subgame beginning with a good history, the minimum incentive compatible price can be derived the same way as in section 2.4.1.3 and has to be smaller than the maximum price the investor is willing to pay. Given a δ close enough to unity such a minimum price can be derived and hence a Nash equilibrium can be established for the subgame, which is shown in appendix B.2. Given a Nash equilibrium when history is good, it remains to show that the players' strategies form an equilibrium when history is bad. When history is bad, the originator will always choose e_l in case a claim to all cash flows of project C is sold. The investor will therefore not make an offer to the originator. Turning to the originator, in case history is bad, the investor will not make an offer in the subsequent period and thereafter. The originator will therefore optimize myopically. He should accept the offer in case the payoff from accepting the offer and

[61] Hence again it is assumed that profits are disbursed at the end of every period, losses are compensated by the firm owners.

shirking exceeds the maximum payoff without securitization and choose e_l, reject otherwise and choose e_h. The payoff from accepting the offer and choosing e_l exceeds the payoff without securitization exactly when $P > \tilde{P}$, therefore the strategies form a subgame-perfect equilibrium.

Here again, the price P for the claim to all cash flows of credit C, derived from equations (2.12) and (2.13) in appendix B.2, could be written as $P_{FLP} + \delta \underline{F}^L$ which is the sum of the price for the FLP on a stand-alone basis and the price for the senior security described throughout the preceding analysis. With the price for the senior security being fixed at $\delta \underline{F}^L$ a range for the incentive-compatible price of the FLP can be specified, given δ close enough to unity. Even more interesting, the originator can sell the junior security but retain the senior security. The senior security does not bear any default risk and does not require any regulatory capital ex ante. In the context of the model one can think of the originator buying back the senior security at a price of $\delta \underline{F}^L$ during the securitization process, hence changing the cash position of $\delta \underline{F}^L$ back to a riskless financial claim of the same amount, which leaves the overall payoff unchanged.

Summarizing the results from model 2 further insights on asset securitization can be gained. Given regulatory capital is a scarce resource under the old regulatory regime, selling high quality assets is a promising strategy. In case the moral hazard conflict is severe securitization with FLP retention is preferable to a whole sale structure. Given the same ex ante situation under the new regulatory regime, namely a shortage of regulatory capital, securitization with FLP retention is no longer revenue enhancing, as regulatory capital cannot be freed up. A whole sale can be the preferable choice in case the moral hazard conflict is weak, otherwise selling the FLP is of utmost importance to be able to reduce the level of risk weighted assets and thus to free up regulatory capital. It is demonstrated that, given repeated interaction of market participants, selling the FLP at a reasonable price is feasible, even on a stand-alone basis.

2.5 Discussion of main results and critical issues

The securitization of assets serves several purposes, two of which are funding of investment opportunities and risk transfer. These two motives for asset securitization were analyzed separately each in the same moral hazard setting. An originator faces the need to sell a share or all of his assets due to funding or regulatory constraints and can either choose a whole sale structure or securitization, where securitization refers to a subordination structure (pay-through). Moral hazard arises as the value of the claim to be sold by the originator is a function of the originator's monitoring choice which can be high or low. Given this setup, securitization is able to mitigate the moral hazard conflict in a one-period setting, when a FLP is retained. Retention of the FLP provides the originator with adequate incentives to choose the high effort level as the benefits from monitoring accrue at the originator. The investor's investment in the senior security is fully protected and hence requires the riskless rate only. Contrary, a whole sale structure results in the choice of low monitoring by the originator as gains from the monitoring effort accrue at the investor and the originator is not able to credibly commit to the high monitoring level in a one-period setting. Securitization with FLP retention is preferable to a whole sale structure in case the moral hazard conflict is high, that is in case the price to be attained in a whole sale combined with low monitoring costs is lower than the proceeds from selling the senior security plus the value of the retained FLP less high monitoring costs. These general results hold for all settings analyzed.

When focusing specifically on regulatory risk transfer needs, the old and the new regulatory regime are considered. Concerning the new regulatory regime, the actually proposed 5% vertical slice rule is not considered in the analysis: while the moral hazard conflict will be less severe, it must not necessarily disappear. Given the moral hazard conflict prevails despite a 5% vertical retention, the game structure in general would be equivalent to the one chosen here. For Basel I, commonly known incentives for regulatory capital arbitrage—selling high quality assets and engaging in low quality assets—are captured in the model. Concerning the new regulatory regime, selling only the senior claim in a securitization transaction still solves the moral hazard conflict, but does not lead to a regulatory capital relief in this model and thus not change the originator's overall position. Hence, especially under the Basel II regime, but for the Basel I regime and the case of refinancing needs as well, selling the FLP can enhance the originator's payoff in case he is able to credibly commit to choose the high level of monitoring and thus able to achieve an appropriate price when bargaining with the investor.

For the case of funding needs, the first-best solution could be realized in the one-period game by imposing a state-dependent fine on the originator, as the originator's effort choice is verifiable ex post in case the bad state is realized. However, such a solution is not feasible when the transaction is driven by risk transfer needs, as the structure would not qualify for regulatory capital relief. Further, SPV structures comprise no recourse clauses, which implies that state-dependent fines are not common in real-world securitizations. Therefore, an alternative mechanism that might be capable to explain the sale of first loss positions despite the existence of the moral hazard conflict was analyzed, relying on the repeated interaction of market participants. When the stage game is repeated, an incentive compatible price for the FLP can be derived for both the case of refinancing needs and the Basel II regime. It can be seen that the FLP can indeed be sold in securitization transactions with the originator nevertheless choosing the high level of monitoring. Furthermore, the senior security and the FLP can trade separately, with the senior security trading at the discounted notional. The price of the FLP depends on the bargaining power of the originator and the investor and must on the one hand exceed an incentive compatible price, but on the other hand guarantee a minimum return for the investor which implies an upper price limit. In case the originator needs to raise fresh money, the senior security will naturally be sold. Given the new investment opportunity is, opposed to the assumption chosen in the model setup, limited in size, securitization of the senior security only can be sufficient to raise the required capital, a possible price discount on the FLP can therefore be avoided when there is some bargaining power with the investor. In case the originator faces a shortage of regulatory capital under the new regulatory regime, selling the senior security is not revenue enhancing. The senior security can be retained without changing the overall payoff of the originator, while the FLP must be sold to achieve regulatory capital relief.

Overall, selling the FLP is value creating in all settings as more NPV positive projects receive funding by the originator, and it is (by assumption) only the originator who has access to the projects to be funded.

There are two critical issues directly related to the model. First, given the choice of e_h the high asset value F^H is reached with certainty as e_h equals one, which implies ex post verifiability of the effort choice given a low outcome is realized. As state-dependent contracts imposing a fine on the originator are not common in securitization and furthermore preclude regulatory capital relief, there is no need to relax the assumption on e_h. However, given some $e_h < 1$ an equilibrium could still be established using review strategies as proposed in Radner (1985).

Second, the assumption of one and the same investor and originator interacting repeatedly might be too simplistic. For the part of the originator, when thinking of a large financial institution as originator of a CLO, a repeated use of the securitization market seems realistic, as securitization is a helpful instrument in various contexts (funding, risk management, regulatory capital requirements). Continuous access to the market for asset securitization is hence valuable.[62] Considering the investor, it is not obvious that one and the same investor will act repeatedly on the market. However, in case investors act only short-term, several investors could be considered acting one after another. In the repeated game, the reputation is maintained by the originator by not defaulting on the FLP. As highlighted, the FLP can trade separately from other securities of the structure, which is commonly the case in reality, and the repeated game can therefore be specified for the FLP alone. To externals, the market for equity pieces is opaque, but according to anecdotic evidence, the number of players in the market on the investors' side is limited. It can there-

[62] This might be less true in case the sponsor is a collateral manager of a CDO who does not originate assets but only assembles assets for a managed transaction, with the only transaction motive being arbitrage. However, additional agency conflicts may arise in such a structure such as risk-shifting in case the FLP is retained, therefore the above model cannot be easily applied to a managed CDO.

fore be argued that market participants on the buy-side for equity pieces are well informed on the performance of past transactions of a specific originator involving the sale of the FLP, which is enforced by the fact that single equity pieces are frequently bought by several investors. Incorporating this argument technically in the above analysis would imply a long run player, the originator, facing short run players, with Shapiro (1982) providing an analysis for such a game structure.

On a general level it must be stated that the model does not attempt to give an explanation for the originator's ability to generate excess returns ($r_C > r_f$, $\gamma > r_f$). As it is not the objective of this analysis to delve deeper into the existence of financial intermediaries but to focus on security design only, the assumptions on r_f, r_C, and γ seem justified.

Also on a general level, the optimal security design involves the decision on two prevalent structural elements: pooling and tranching. The model developed here only focuses on tranching, possible benefits arising from pooling are not incorporated in the analysis. Pooling involves the bundling of several underlying assets. The pooling of assets reduces the variance of payoffs due to diversification and can be utility enhancing as shown in e.g. Riddiough (1997) and DeMarzo (2005). However, pooling is not necessary to proof the marketability of the FLP in the above moral hazard setting and thus not included in the analysis.

Furthermore, it was illustrated that the retention of the FLP in the one-period game protects investors of the senior security and hence serves as credit enhancement. FLP retention is the only credit enhancement incorporated in the model, however, real world securitization structures commonly are more complex and include additional internal credit enhancements such as overcollateralization and the creation of a reserve account but also differentiated rules on the allocation of losses. Incorporating overcollateralization into the model is equivalent to a retained first loss position. Integrating loss allocation rules and the creation of a reserve account would however require a multi-period stage game, a possible venue for future research.[63]

[63] See Hein (2006) for a simulation-based analysis of different credit enhancements.

A last remark is given concerning the maturity of the securities issued in the model. In the above analysis, the maturity of the securities issued matches perfectly with the maturity of the underlying credit C. Actual distortions in the ABS market that rose due to term transformations pursued in so called *Conduit* and *SIV* structures hence cannot arise in the model lined out above.[64]

2.6 Conclusion

In this analysis, a relationship lender is considered who has access to a new investment opportunity but either needs to raise funding or faces a shortage of regulatory capital, and therefore structures a CLO. This originator is not able to sell the FLP in a one-period game due to moral hazard. The model derived above shows that reputation effects can mitigate moral hazard and explain the sale of the FLP in securitization transactions. An issuer, who benefits from a regular interaction with the market for equity pieces, will not shirk on his monitoring effort to preserve future access to this market, with the importance of the market for equity positions being reinforced by the new regulatory regime. The sale of the FLP despite moral hazard can hence also be explained without relying on the existence of sophisticated investors.

While market participants emphasize reputation effects, empirical evidence is limited. Ambrose / LaCour-Little / Sanders (2005) as well as Cantor and Hu (2007) present evidence for the importance of reputation in the securitization market. As there is so far no information on the sale or retention of equity pieces, issues related to the above model have not been considered in empirical research. In June 2008 Fitch proposed to increase transparency on FLP retention.[65] Given such a procedure would be accepted by market participants and hence the whereabouts of first loss pieces common knowledge, I suspect the following hypotheses, based on the importance of reputation effects in the model derived above, to hold:

---

[64] The German IKB and their vehicle Rhineland Funding is a prominent example for a bank that provided liquidity guarantees which were beyond their reach on revolving short-term notes issued in a Conduit structure.

[65] See Fitch Ratings (2008).

1. The first originators to issue first loss positions had a successful track record on previous securitization transactions.

2. The performance of balance sheet CLOs that comprise the sale of the FLP will not systematically differ from the performance of balance sheet CLOs where the FLP was retained. Performance addresses any tranche including the FLP.

3. First loss pieces will be sold in future despite the actual financial crisis that was triggered by the securitization of subprime mortgages.

4. In the long run successful issuers of first loss positions will be those who have a long-term interest in the ability to sell the FLP. Theses are especially commercial banks, who engage in balance sheet transactions not for securitization's sake but for various causes such as risk management, regulatory capital management, and funding. For sponsors such as asset managers of CDOs securitization is an end in itself, and the primary focus is on short-term arbitrage profits. These sponsors are predicted to be less successful on the market for equity pieces than long-term players such as commercial banks.

5. On a general level punishment is expected to function: issuers that failed to service a transaction appropriately will not be capable to access the market for future transactions.

The actual crisis is expected to accelerate market learning, and, given that hypothesis five holds, drive out bad quality from the market. This effect is desirable, as it would reanimate the market for asset securitization, which is associated with several positive functions despite the actual crisis and its severe negative impact. For a medium term perspective, the 5% vertical slice rule proposed by the European Commission might hence be obsolete given sufficient transparency can be established on the so far opaque market.

Appendix for chapter 2

Appendix A: Existence of equilibria in the repeated game – model 1

It is to show that there exists at least a δ for which the minimum price that is necessary to induce the high monitoring effort is lower than the maximum price the investor is wiling to pay, hence

$$\frac{S}{1+\gamma}+\frac{c(e_h)}{1+\gamma}+(c(e_h)-c(e_l))\frac{1-\delta}{\delta(1+\gamma)(1-e_l)}<\delta C(1+i)\ . \tag{2.10}$$

Assume first that $\delta > 0$ (which is always true with $r_f > 0$). Inequality (2.10) can then be written as the following quadratic inequality:

$$\begin{aligned}\delta^2(1+\gamma)(1-e_l)(C(1+i)-F^L)-\delta[(C(1+i)-F^L)(1-e_l)-\\ (c(e_h)-c(e_l))]-(c(e_h)-c(e_l))>0\ .\end{aligned} \tag{2.11}$$

Define the following parameters a, b and c:

$$\begin{aligned}a &\equiv (1+\gamma)(1-e_l)(C(1+i)-F^L)\\ b &\equiv [(C(1+i)-F^L)(1-e_l)-(c(e_h)-c(e_l))]\\ c &\equiv (c(e_h)-c(e_l))\end{aligned}$$

Inequality (2.11) holds for the following parameter values of δ:

$$\begin{aligned}\delta_1 &> \sqrt{\frac{c}{a}+\left(\frac{1}{2}\frac{b}{a}\right)^2}+\frac{1}{2}\frac{b}{a}=\delta^*\\ \delta_2 &< -\sqrt{\frac{c}{a}+\left(\frac{1}{2}\frac{b}{a}\right)^2}+\frac{1}{2}\frac{b}{a}\end{aligned}$$

It can be seen that δ_2 will always be negative and can hence be excluded, while δ^* will always be positive. It remains to verify that δ^* is smaller than one, hence that

$$\sqrt{\frac{c}{a}+\left(\frac{1}{2}\frac{b}{a}\right)^2}+\frac{1}{2}\frac{b}{a}<1 ,$$

which reduces to

$$\gamma(1-e_l)(C(1+i)-F^L)>0$$

which is always satisfied. Therefore, there exists at least one $\delta<1$ for which inequality (2.10) holds which proofs the existence of a Nash equilibrium in the infinitely repeated game.

For $\delta<0$ a second solution to inequality (2.10) can be found. In that case, the sign in inequality (2.11) changes, and the following parameter range satisfies the resulting inequality:

$$-\sqrt{\frac{c}{a}+\left(\frac{1}{2}\frac{b}{a}\right)^2}+\frac{1}{2}\frac{b}{a}<\delta<0 .$$

However, as δ must exceed zero to obtain an economically reasonable result, the only δ which supports inequality (2.10) is any $\delta>\delta^*$.

Appendix B: Analysis of the repeated game in the regulatory context – model 2

Appendix B.1: Derivation of the threshold $\tilde{P}$

The threshold $\tilde{P}$ is the critical price for which accepting the investor's offer and acting myopically yields the same equity payoff to the originator as declining the offer and realizing the payoff that results from not selling project C:

$$\frac{P-\delta c(e_l)-\underline{F}^L}{rw_G^{BII}\cdot 8\%}(\gamma-r_f)+P(1+r_f)-c(e_l)-\underline{F}^L(1+r_f)=$$
$$=C(1+i)-c(e_h)-\underline{F}^L(1+r_f)$$

$\tilde{P}$ thus levels at:

$$\tilde{P}=\frac{C(1+i)-c(e_h)+c(e_l)+\frac{(\delta c(e_l)+\underline{F}^L)(\gamma-r_f)}{rw_G^{BII}\cdot 8\%}}{1+r_f+\frac{(\gamma-r_f)}{rw_G^{BII}\cdot 8\%}}$$

Note that $\tilde{P}$ naturally resembles to the threshold $P>(C(1+i)-c(e_h)+c(e_l))/(1+\gamma)$ derived in section 2.4.1.3, however differs due to the impact of P on the regulatory capital.

Appendix B.2: Existence of equilibria in the repeated game – model 2

Analog to appendix A it is to show that there exists at least a δ for which the minimum price that is necessary to induce the high monitoring effort is lower than the maximum price the investor is willing to pay.

The minimum incentive compatible price P_{min} is derived from comparing the (equity) payoffs from sticking to the equilibrium path with those that result from a deviation from the equilibrium path, where the investor's punishment strategy is to retreat from the market.

Given a price P and the choice of e_h by the originator, the value of the originator's equity levels at:

$$V_{e_h}=\frac{1}{1-\delta}\left[\frac{P-\delta c(e_h)-\underline{F}^L}{rw_G^{BII}\cdot 8\%}(\gamma-r_f)+P(1+r_f)-c(e_h)-\underline{F}^L(1+r_f)\right]\ . \tag{2.12}$$

In case the originator shirks and chooses e_l, the low asset value will be reached with probability $(1-e_l)$ and trigger the punishment, therefore the firm value levels at:

$$V_{e_l} = \frac{P-\delta c(e_l)-\underline{F}^L}{rw_G^{BII}\cdot 8\%}(\gamma - r_f)+P(1+r_f)-c(e_l)-\underline{F}^L(1+r_f)+ \\ e_l\delta V_{e_l}+(1-e_l)\frac{\delta}{1-\delta}(C(1+i)-c(e_h)-\underline{F}^L(1+r_f)) \ . \tag{2.13}$$

Note that in the regulatory setting, shirking not only reduces monitoring costs but also has a positive impact on the $t=0^+$ available regulatory capital due to higher short-term revenues.

Knowing the payoffs from the high and the low effort level the minimum incentive compatible price P_{min} can be derived from setting $V_{e_h} > V_{e_l}$ and levels at:

$$\begin{aligned} P_{min} &> \{rw_G^{BII}\cdot 8\%\left[(c(e_h)-c(e_l))(1-\delta)+(1-e_l)\delta C(1+i)\right]- \\ &- \delta(\gamma - r_f)\left[(c(e_l)-c(e_h))+\left[e_l(\delta c(e_h)+\underline{F}^L)-(\delta c(e_l)+\underline{F}^L)\right]\right]\} \\ &/ \left[\delta(1-e_l)((1+r_f)rw_G^{BII}\cdot 8\%+\gamma-r_f)\right] \ . \end{aligned}$$

Note that this expression for the minimum price is not defined for two parameter values of r_f. In case r_f would take the value of -1, δ is not defined. In case r_f would take the value of $(\gamma + rw_G^{BII}\cdot 8\%)/(1-rw_G^{BII}\cdot 8\%)$ the denominator would equal zero and the expression be thus not defined either. However, as r_f exceeds zero by definition and as $(\gamma + rw_G^{BII}\cdot 8\%)/(1-rw_G^{BII}\cdot 8\%)$ is always bigger than γ, these extreme values are of no further concern.

Given the price exceeds P_{min} the originator is induced to choose the high effort level. Such a price will however only be acceptable to the investor in case he can realize a return which exceeds the risk free rate, which implies a maximum price the investor is willing to pay for a claim to all cash flows of project C. As the investor receives a payoff of $C(1+i)$ in $t=1$ when purchasing all cash flows from project C, the maximum price is determined by

$$\frac{C(1+i)-P_{max}}{P_{max}} > r_f \tag{2.14}$$

and levels at $P_{max} < \delta C(1+i)$. For the existence of an equilibrium there hence has to be at least a δ that satisfies $P_{min} < P_{max}$. The existence of such a δ is shown in the following. Remember that δ equals $1/(1+r_f)$ so that the minimum and the maximum price can be written as functions of r_f and that $0 < r_f < \gamma$ must hold. Evaluating $P_{max}(r_f)$ and $P_{min}(r_f)$ at these boundaries for r_f reveals that $P_{max}(r_f=0) > P_{min}(r_f=0)$ and that $P_{max}(r_f=\gamma) < P_{min}(r_f=\gamma)$. As both $P_{min}(r_f)$ and $P_{max}(r_f)$ are continuous on the interval $0 < r_f < \gamma$, $P_{min}(r_f)$ and $P_{max}(r_f)$ must intersect at least once on the relevant interval. Now setting $P_{min}(r_f) < P_{max}(r_f)$ results in a quadratic inequality:

$$xr_f^2 + yr_f + z > 0 \ , \tag{2.15}$$

with the parameters x, y, and z being:

$$\begin{aligned}
x &\equiv (c(e_h)-c(e_l))(1-rw_G^{BII}\cdot 8\%)+(1-e_l)\underline{F}^L \\
y &\equiv (1-e_l)(\underline{F}^L(1-\gamma)-C(1+i)+c(e_h))-(c(e_h)-c(e_l))(\gamma+rw_G^{BII}\cdot 8\%) \\
z &\equiv \gamma(1-e_l)(C(1+i)-\underline{F}^L-c(e_h)) \ .
\end{aligned}$$

First, for $-z/x+(y/2x)^2 < 0$, inequality (2.15) would be satisfied for any value of r_f. For the more interesting case of $-z/x+(y/2x)^2 \geq 0$, the quadratic inequality (2.15) is satisfied for the following parameter values of r_f:

$$\begin{aligned}
r_1 &> \sqrt{-\frac{z}{x}+\left(\frac{1}{2}\frac{y}{x}\right)^2}-\frac{1}{2}\frac{y}{x} \\
r_2 &< -\sqrt{-\frac{z}{x}+\left(\frac{1}{2}\frac{y}{x}\right)^2}-\frac{1}{2}\frac{y}{x}
\end{aligned}$$

It remains to verify that r_1 and r_2 are feasible solutions, i.e. it has to be shown that $0 < r_{1,2} < \gamma$ holds.

Considering r_1 first, r_1 can only be a feasible solution in case r_1 takes values smaller than γ, which can be written as:

$$\sqrt{-\frac{z}{x}+\left(\frac{1}{2}\frac{y}{x}\right)^2} < \frac{1}{2}\frac{y}{x}+\gamma \ . \tag{2.16}$$

For the further analysis, two cases need to be distinguished.

Case 1.1: $\frac{y}{2x}+\gamma<0$

For $\frac{y}{2x}+\gamma<0$ the LHS of equation (2.16) will always exceed the RHS, therefore equation (2.16) cannot be satisfied.

Case 1.2: $\frac{y}{2x}+\gamma>0$

For $\frac{y}{2x}+\gamma>0$ the inequality can be written as $x\gamma^2+y\gamma+z>0$ and reduces to

$$-\gamma(c(e_h)-c(e_l))rw_G^{BII}\cdot 8\%(\gamma+1)>0$$

which is never satisfied. Therefore r_1 is greater than γ and can be excluded as solution.

Considering r_2, r_2 equally can only be a feasible solution in case r_2 takes values smaller than γ, which can be written as:

$$-\sqrt{-\frac{z}{x}+\left(\frac{1}{2}\frac{y}{x}\right)^2} < \frac{1}{2}\frac{y}{x}+\gamma \ . \tag{2.17}$$

Again, the two cases need to be considered.

Case 2.1: $\frac{y}{2x}+\gamma<0$

For $\frac{y}{2x}+\gamma<0$ equation (2.17) can be written as $x\gamma^2+y\gamma+z<0$ which reduces to

$$-\gamma(c(e_h)-c(e_l))rw_G^{BII}\cdot 8\%(\gamma+1)<0$$

and is always satisfied.

Case 2.2: $\frac{y}{2x}+\gamma>0$

For $\frac{y}{2x}+\gamma>0$ the LHS of equation (2.17) will always be smaller than the RHS. Hence, r_2 takes values smaller than γ.

Furthermore, r_2 must take values greater than zero to be a feasible solution. Setting $r_2>0$ reduces to

$$-\gamma(1-e_l)(C(1+i)-\underline{F}^L-c(e_h))<0$$

which is always satisfied due to assumption A.2 combined with the fact that $\underline{F}^L<C$.

Hence, only r_2 is a feasible solution for the repeated game setting given the new regulatory framework. Defining

$$\delta^{**}=\frac{1}{1+r_2}\ ,$$

equilibria in the repeated game can be supported for any $\delta>\delta^{**}$.

Bibliography for chapter 2

Amato, Jeffery / Remolona, Eli (2005): The pricing of unexpected credit losses, Working Paper No. 190, Bank for International Settlements, Basel.

Ambrose, Brent / LaCour-Little, Michael / Sanders, Anthony (2005): Does regulatory capital arbitrage, reputation, or asymmetric information drive securitization?, in: *Journal of Financial Services Research*, Vol. 28, pp. 113–133.

Basel Committee on Banking Supervision (1988): International convergence of capital measurement and capital standards, Basel.

Basel Committee on Banking Supervision (2004): International convergence of capital measurement and capital standards – A revised framework, Basel.

Becker, Claas (2006): Transfer mittelständischer Kreditrisiken, in: *Zeitschrift für das gesamte Kreditwesen*, Vol. 21, pp. 1151–1153.

Becker, Claas (2007): Kapitalmarktorientierte Preisbildung für illiquide Mittelstandskredite, in: *Zeitschrift für das gesamte Kreditwesen*, Vol. 14, pp. 721–724.

Benzschawel, Terry / Fok, Henry (2006): A look at CDO equity in a portfolio context: A yield enhance, diversifier, in: *Journal of Structured Finance*, Vol. 12, pp. 37–54.

Bhattacharya, Anand / Fabozzi, Frank (1996): Asset-Backed Securities, New Hope, Pennsylvania.

Bhattacharya, Sudipto / Boot, Arnound / Thakor, Anjan (1998): The economics of bank regulation, in: *Journal of Money, Credit, and Banking*, Vol. 30, pp. 745–770.

Bluhm, Christian / Overbeck, Ludger / Wagner, Christoph (2003): An introduction to credit risk modeling, London.

Bluhm, Christian / Overbeck, Ludger (2007): Structured credit portfolio analysis, baskets & CDOs, London.

Boot, Arnoud / Thakor, Anjan (1993): Security design, in: *Journal of Finance*, Vol. 48, pp. 1349–1378.

Brennan, Michael / Hein, Julia / Poon, Ser-Huang (2008): Tranching and pooling, Working Paper, UCLA.

Bundesaufsichtsamt für das Kreditwesen (2002): Behandlung einbehaltener First Loss Tranchen im Rahmen synthetischer ABS-Transaktionen im Grundsatz I, Bonn.

Cantor, Richard / Hu, Jian (2007): Deal sponsor and credit risk of asset-backed and mortgage-backed securities, Working Paper.

Commison of the European Communities (2008): Proposal for a directive of the European parliament and of the coucil amending directives 2006/48/EC and 2006/49/EC as regards banks affiliated to central institutions, certain own funds items, large exposures, supervisory arrangements, and crisis management, Brussels.

DeMarzo, Peter / Duffie, Darell (1999): A liquidity-based model of security design, in: *Econometrica*, Vol. 67, pp. 65–99.

DeMarzo, Peter (2005): The pooling and tranching of securities: A model of informed intermediation, in: *Review of Financial Studies*, Vol. 18, pp. 1–35.

Dewatripont, Mathias / Tirole, Jean (1994): The prudential regulation of banks, Cambridge, Massachusetts.

Diamond, Douglas W. (1984): Financial intermediation and delegated monitoring, in: *The Review of Economic Studies*, Vol. 51, pp. 393–414.

Elsas, Ralf / Krahnen, Jan Pieter (2004): Universal banks and relationships with firms, in: The German Financial System, edited by: Krahnen, Jan Pieter and Schmidt, Reinhard H. (**2004**), pp. 197–232.

Elton, Edwin / Gruber, Martin / Agrawal, Deepak / Mann, Christopher (2001): Explaining the rate spread on corporate bonds, in: *Journal of Finance*, Vol. 56, pp. 247–277.

Emse, Cordula (2005): Forderungsverbriefungen und ihre regulatorische Erfassung, zeb, Münster.

Financial Services Authority (2001): The interim prudential sourcebook banks, SE, section 9, London.

Fitch Ratings (2002): Going public with private equity CFOs, New York.

Fitch Ratings (2005): Hedge funds: An emerging force in the global credit markets, New York.

Fitch Ratings (2006): Accounting for servicer concentration in CDOs, New York.

Fitch Ratings (2008): Exposure draft: Retaining equity piece risk – Enhancing transparency, New York.

Franke, Günter / Krahnen, Jan Pieter (2008): The future of securitization, CFS Working Paper No. 2008/31.

Fudenberg, Drew / Tirole, Jean (1991): Game theory, Cambridge, Massachusetts.

Gaur, Vishal / Seshadri, Sridhar / Subrahmanyam, Marti (2003): Market incompleteness and super value additivity: Implications for securitization, Working Paper, Stern School of Business, New York.

Gibbons, Robert (1992): A primer in game theory, Hertfordshire.

Gorton, Gary / Pennacchi, George (1995): Banks and loan sales: Marketing nonmarketable assets, in: *Journal of Monetary Economics*, Vol. 35, pp. 389–411.

Gorton, Gary / Souleles, Nicholas (2005): Special purpose vehicles and securitization, Working Paper, Wharton School, Pennsylvania.

Hein, Julia (2006): Optimization of credit enhancements in collateralized loan obligations: The role of loss allocation and reserve account, Working Paper, University of Konstanz.

Hofmann, Bernd / Pluto, Katja (2005): Zentrale Aspekte der neuen aufsichtlichen Eigenmittelanforderungen (Basel II), in: *Schmalenbachs Zeitschrift für betriebswirtschaftliche Forschung*, Vol. 52 (Sonderheft), pp. 241–270.

International Monetary Fund (2006): Global financial stability report. Market developments and issues, Washington D.C., April 2006.

Jensen, Michael / Meckling, William (1976): Theory of the firm: Managerial behavior, agency costs and ownership structure, in: *Journal of Financial Economics*, Vol. 3, pp. 305–360.

Jobst, Andreas (2002): Collateralised Loan Obligations (CLOs) – A primer, Working Paper No. 2002/13, Center for Financial Studies.

Jones, David (2000): Emerging problems with the Basel Capital Accord: Regulatory capital arbitrage and related issues, in: *Journal of Banking and Finance*, Vol. 24, pp. 35–58.

Krahnen, Jan Pieter (2005): Der Handel von Kreditrisiken: Eine neue Dimension des Kapitalmarktes, in: *Perspektiven der Wirtschaftspolitik*, Vol. 6, pp. 499–519.

Merchant, Shanker (2004): The CDO equity: An emerging class of alternative investments, in: *Journal of Alternative Investments*, Vol. 7, Winter 2004, pp. 47–58.

Nell, Martin / Richter, Andreas (2004): Improving risk allocation through indexed cat bonds, in: *Geneva Papers on Risk and Insurance*, Vol. 29, pp. 183–201.

Ohl, Hans-Peter (**1994**): Asset Backed Securities, Wiesbaden.

Paul, Stephan (**1994**): Bankenintermediation und Verbriefung – Neue Chancen und Risiken für Kreditinstitute durch Asset Backed Securities?, Wiesbaden.

Plantin, Guillaume (**2004**): Tranching, Working Paper, Tepper School of Business, Pennsylvania.

Radner, Roy (**1985**): Repeated principal-agent games with discounting, in: *Econometrica*, Vol. 53, pp. 1173–1198.

Ricken, Stephan (**2007**): Kreditrisikotransfer europäischer Banken – Theoretische Begründungsansätze und ihre kapitalmarktempirische Überprüfung anhand von Verbriefungstransaktionen, Frankfurt a.M.

Riddiough, Timothy (**1997**): Optimal design and governance of asset-backed securities, in: *Journal of Financial Intermediation*, Vol. 6, pp. 121–153.

Rudolph, Bernd (**2006**): Unternehmensfinanzierung und Kapialmarkt, Tübingen.

Rudolph, Bernd / Hofmann, Bernd / Schaber, Albert / Schäfer, Klaus (**2007**): Kreditrisikotransfer – Moderne Instrumente und Methoden, Berlin.

Shapiro, Carl (**1982**): Consumer information, product quality and seller reputation, in: *Bell Journal of Economics*, Vol. 13, pp. 20–35.

Shapiro, Carl / Stiglitz, Joseph (**1984**): Equilibrium unemployment as a worker discipline device, in: *American Economic Review*, Vol. 74, pp. 433–444.

Watterson, Paul (**2005**): The evolution of the CDO squared, in: *Journal of Structured Finance*, Vol. 11, pp. 6–12.

3 Combination notes: Market segmentation and equity transfer

3.1 Introduction

Securitization of assets can be characterized by two prevailing structural elements. Several assets are assembled (pooling) to collateralize securities, which in turn are sold to financial markets in different tranches (tranching) with the principle of subordination usually being applied. The resulting notes are called asset backed securities (ABS). Securitization grew tremendously in the last decade, with different types of assets being securitized. The main categories are the securitization of mortgages (RMBS, CMBS), the securitization of consumer assets, and the securitization of debt claims (CDOs).[1] The analysis presented in this chapter focuses on one special note issued in securitization transactions: combination notes (also called combo notes). A combination note (CN) is constructed by combining parts of two or more tranches of a securitization transaction.[2] Usually, but not in every case, a CN comprises a share of the first loss piece (FLP), which is the most junior security of a securitization transaction, also known as the equity piece or junior security.[3] The creation of combination notes is not part of the original structuring process; rather, 'plain vanilla' tranches are created first given the estimated portfolio loss distribution of the

[1] The securitization of consumer assets is sometimes referred to as ABS, such as the securitization of assets in general.

[2] According to Standard & Poor's (2002), p. 143, CNs can also comprise parts of tranches of different deals, which however was not observed for any CN in the data used here. A structure that was observed three out of 398 times was the combination of equity with OATs (obligation assimilable du trésor, a French government bond).

[3] Tavakoli (2003), pp. 202-204 further distinguishes participation notes from combination notes, where participation notes are defined as notes that comprise a share of the equity position, and combination notes are defined to be a combination of parts of rated tranches. This distinction is not made in the following, and was not found in any other source.

underlying asset portfolio, and combination notes result from combining parts of two or more of the 'plain vanilla' tranches after their structure has been determined. Furthermore, most CNs carry a rating assigned by one of the dominating rating agencies, and their existence is observed by market participants.

If capital markets were perfect and complete, neither combination notes nor securitization in general could add value to a firm. But market frictions exist, which can make securitization and also the creation of combination notes value creating.[4] From an originator's point of view, securitization in general can serve three main purposes: raising funds, risk transfer, and arbitrage. Considering combination notes in particular, several of these motivations might drive their issuance. Combination notes possibly facilitate equity transfer, which becomes more important due to the new regulatory framework Basel II.[5] But also asset managers who issue managed CDO transactions and are not necessarily regulated under Basel II will prefer to transfer equity rather than to retain it. On the one hand, asset managers' capital is limited. Selling a share of the FLP allows them to structure larger transactions and thus to increase their leverage or to increase their turnover. On the other hand, asset managers generate a substantial part of their income via fees, and therefore will prefer to transfer equity risk to market participants. From an investor's perspective, combination notes can facilitate access to a certain risk-return profile, which might otherwise not be accessible due to investment restrictions, be they internal or external. Combination notes allow investors to participate in the residual income of securitization transactions, with the investment usually being rated at least at investment

---

4 See Bluhm / Overbeck / Wagner (2003), pp. 253-263 for a detailed description of originator and investor benefits of CDOs, Merchant (2004) for an introduction to the investor's point of view on CDO equity, and Brennan / Hein / Poon (2008) for an analysis of arbitrage CDOs.

5 Under the new regulatory framework ("International Convergence of Capital Management and Capital Standards - A Revised Framework"), the distorting incentives to sell high quality assets while retaining low quality assets were mitigated in order to stop regulatory capital arbitrage. See Basel Committee on Banking Supervision (2004), §§ 538-643, for the treatment of securitization transactions. As a result, selling the FLP has become more common in recent years; see International Monetary Fund (2006), p. 56 and Fitch Ratings (2005), p. 6. The extent to which equity pieces have been sold is so far unknown to regulators, though greater transparency is discussed by market participants; see Fitch Ratings (2008).

grade, and the risk often being concentrated in the interest stream of the note but not in the principal amount.

While the above motives drive securitization in the market, their security design has been addressed in several theoretical contributions focusing on transaction costs, market incompleteness, and asymmetric information. To begin with, pooling of assets can reduce costs when the trading of individual loans is costly.[6] Gaur / Seshadri / Subrahmanyam (2003) analyze market incompleteness and focus on a market where some but not all assets can be priced uniquely. They show that singling out new cash flow profiles increases market spanning, which is rewarded by a premium. Their results apply to securitization, where the optimal structure arises from the issuer's optimization. Problems due to information asymmetries can arise both ex ante and ex post. Ex ante, the originator can be tempted to choose a poor average asset quality for the underlying asset pool, which bears the risk of adverse selection and hence market failure. Articles focusing on ex ante asymmetries are Boot / Thakor (1993), Riddiough (1997), DeMarzo (2005), and Plantin (2004). Ex post, investors of securitization transactions face moral hazard in case the value of the asset pool is a function of the originator's unobservable monitoring activity. Articles focusing on ex post asymmetries include Gorton / Pennacchi (1995), Gorton / Souleles (2005), and also the model presented in chapter 2. One stylized result of most of the above articles is the suggestion to originators to retain the first loss piece in order to either send an appropriate signal to the market concerning asset pool quality in an adverse selection setting, or to provide the originator with the required incentives to mitigate moral hazard. The need to retain the FLP is relaxed in Plantin (2004) and in the model presented in chapter 2. Plantin (2004) is the first to point out explicitly that the FLP can be sold to sophisticated investors in case information production on the FLP is profitable to them—a result in line with Boot and Thakor (1993) but more specifically tailored to securitization transactions. I use a repeated game argument in chapter 2 to show that, even though the FLP is not retained, incentives to monitor the FLP can be maintained for the originator in a moral hazard setting.

6 See Duffie / Gârleanu (2001), p. 42, for a short discussion on transaction costs.

Given that combination notes commonly comprise a share of the FLP, this article is the first to analyze observed equity transfer in asset securitization empirically. Existing empirical evidence on securitization is still scarce, with Firla-Cuchra / Jenkinson (2005), Firla-Cuchra (2005), and Franke / Weber (2007) being the most important contributions for this research.[7] Firla-Cuchra / Jenkinson (2005) focus on the impact of market segmentation and asymmetric information on tranching and pricing of ABS, while Firla-Cuchra (2005) focuses on launch spreads only. Franke / Weber (2007) strongly focus on the impact of the underlying assets' quality on structural choices of CDO transactions such as the size of the FLP, the number of tranches, and the choice between true sale and synthetic structures. To my knowledge, combination notes so far have not been subject to closer examination, neither from academia nor from market participants. The purpose of this analysis is to explore the properties of combination notes empirically in the context of existing evidence. Combination notes are interesting for various reasons. First, given that combination notes commonly comprise some share of the first loss piece, equity transfer can be estimated. Second, rating of combination notes requires a closer examination, as the underlying share of equity is commonly not rated and rating methodologies vary for combination notes. Third, the tranching decision on combination notes can yield important insights. It can provide evidence whether combination notes seem to be strongly demand-driven, i.e. are structured to cater segmented markets, or equally reduce information asymmetries. Fourth, the structuring decision of the overall deal can reveal whether combination notes are used as equity transfer vehicles. Fifth, the analysis of launch spreads can reveal whether the presence of combination notes has an impact on the pricing of securitization transactions. And sixth, combination notes are complex securities, and provide a venue for an analysis of the success of financial innovations.

The analysis presented in this chapter is unique, as it is the first analysis of combination notes, based on a manually collected dataset. It is also the first article to shed some light on equity piece issuance, as general data on the distri-

---

[7] For an extended version of Franke / Weber (2007) in English language see Franke / Hermann / Weber (2007).

bution of equity pieces is not available. The chapter is organized as follows. In section 3.2, research questions are formulated. Section 3.3 provides a description of the data and general insights on combination notes. Section 3.4 contains the empirical analysis. Section 3.5 concludes with a summary of major results.

3.2 Derivation of hypotheses on the structuring and impact of combination notes

The research questions formulated in this section can be grouped into two major blocks. One block addresses the question of the extent to which combination notes are tailored to investor needs and hence cater to segmented markets, or if they equally resolve information asymmetries. The other block focuses on the risk transfer associated with combination notes. A minor research question focuses on the success of financial innovations, with CNs being an example for complex securities issued only in recent years. Different *explorative* hypotheses are outlined in the following.

Combination notes are securities that have special risk return properties and might face markets that are not very deep. The existence of limited demand capacity can make tranching beneficial as it might reduce price discounts or might even be necessary to market CNs at all. Additionally, limited demand capacity might also place an upper bound on the transferability of equity of a single deal. This leads to the following hypotheses:

> *H1*: The number of combination notes increases with the absolute combination note volume in the deal.
>
> *H2*: The relative size of the combination notes in a deal will be negatively related to the overall size of the deal.

Taken together, H1 and H2 also imply a rather constant size of each single combination note. Aside from this, it can be suspected that combination notes will carry a rating of at least investment grade, which will be elaborated in section 3.3. If combination notes were structured to reduce asymmetric information, combination notes should be tranched more heavily where information asymmetries are higher, which leads to hypothesis 3:

H3: The number of new rating classes added to the original number of rating classes by structuring combination notes will increase with increasing information asymmetries.

Rating classes is a term first introduced by Firla-Cuchra / Jenkinson (2005) and is the number of differently rated tranches in a deal. The difference between the overall number of tranches of a deal and the number of rating classes is called *market classes*, i.e. tranches that do not provide new information in terms of rating to capital markets and that are primarily structured to be marketable.[8] However, as the plain vanilla tranches are structured first, their tranching should reveal most information on the underlying loss distribution, and their repackaging in a combination note is not expected to release additional information on the loss distribution. Therefore, H3 is expected to be rejected.

Combination notes are a means to transfer equity. It shall hence be analyzed whether risk transfer can be identified as a driver for the structuring and issuance of combination notes. Given that combination notes are constructed to transfer equity risk, combination notes will be especially valuable when the quality of the underlying assets is comparably low and the FLP proportionally large. Furthermore, the share of equity comprised in combination notes cannot be increased arbitrarily in order to preserve marketability of the CN and to be able to obtain a rating on the CN. Selling more equity will therefore require selling a larger combination note. Together, this results in hypothesis 4:

H4: The relative size of the combination notes in a deal will increase with decreasing quality of the underlying assets.

The existence of combination notes is observed by market participants. As the majority of combination notes contain a fraction of the FLP, market participants have reasonable evidence to notice equity transfer. From the market

[8] To take an example, a transaction with two AAA tranches, one AA+ tranche, two AA tranches, one BBB tranche and one not rated FLP has four rating classes and three market classes. Market classes can however differ in other characteristics than rating such as currency and maturity. Throughout the chapter, rating letters according to S&P and Fitch Ratings are used, which could equally be replaced by those of Moody's.

participants' perspective, equity transfer is a positive signal on the deal structure: someone is directing his funds to the most subordinate tranche of the deal, which protects all other tranches issued in the deal. This positive signal can have an impact on pricing, and results in hypothesis 5:

> *H5*: Launch spreads on the plain vanilla tranches decrease with an increase in observed equity transfer.

Combination notes result from combining two or more non-trivial assets, and are therefore themselves complex securities. It can be argued that experience and reputation are necessary to successfully issue financial innovations such as combination notes, which results in hypothesis 6:

> *H6*: Combination notes are issued by experienced institutions with a positive track record on the market.

The above hypotheses will be tested in section 3.4. Given data availability, hypothesis 6 will only be discussed in section 3.3 and not tested in depth. Methodologically, the analysis will follow Firla-Cuchra / Jenkinson (2005) and Firla-Cuchra (2005) wherever possible in order to produce comparable results in this young field of empirical research.

3.3 Data description and combination note properties

3.3.1 General descriptive statistics

I use a unique dataset on European CDO transactions, where the core data is compiled from an internal database at HypoVereinsbank/UniCredit Global Markets, which is fed by different sources such as Moody's, Fitch, Standard & Poor's, Bloomberg, and Reuters. Various variables concerning combination notes were manually collected using pre-sale and new issue reports by Moody's, Standard & Poor's, and Fitch. Overall, 130 deals that comprise 1433 tranches, thereof 406 combination notes, could be identified. The dataset spans a period from July 2002 until September 2007 and should cover the majority of combination notes issued in Europe in that period, although, notes that did not appear

Table 3.1: Asset manager ratings – Asset manager ratings are assembled from Fitch CDO asset manager ratings (CAM ratings) and translated in a numerical value, with seven being the best and one being the worst score.

	Obs	Mean	Std. Dev.
all Fitch CAM ratings	58	4.483	1.442
in dataset by transaction	37	5.270	1.018
in dataset by asset manager	10	4.700	1.160

in any publication cannot be identified. Out of these deals, four were identified as outliers and removed from the data.[9] The data decreases to 126 deals, 1385 tranches, and thereof 398 combination notes. All deals are backed by loans or bonds, with the majority (97) being leveraged loan securitizations, and the remainder being securitizations of ABS, mixed assets, CLOs, high yield bonds, and SME loans. The overall volume of these deals amounts to € 56.6 billion, with € 4.9 billion thereof being equity.[10] Sponsors of these transactions are banks as well as asset managers.

Some information could be gathered on the asset managers involved in the deals. Fitch publishes a CDO asset manager rating (CAM rating). These ratings were assembled for the asset managers involved in the data where available, and translated into a numerical value, ranging from 7 (best) to 1 (worst).[11] These values were compared to all available Fitch CAM ratings, as reported in table

9 The outliers were removed for the following reasons. One deal was, due to super senior swaps, extraordinarily large with a deal volume of € 2.9 billion, which is three times larger than the second biggest deal in the data. One deal is a CFO, hence a securitization of hedge fund and/or private equity assets, that differs remarkably in its structure by having a FLP that covers 38% of the deal volume. Two deals comprise extraordinarily large combination notes that cover 60% and 75% of the deal volume, with the third largest relative CN size being 35%—and being the CFO just mentioned to be excluded as well. The fourth largest relative CN size is at only 24%, so that the exclusion of these outliers seems reasonable.

10 In case tranches have been issued in dollars, the dollar amounts have been converted to euros using the corresponding exchange rate.

11 The exact mapping is as follows: CAM1=7, CAM1−=6, CAM2+=5, CAM2=4, CAM2−=3, CAM3=2 and CAM4=1. Fitch CAM ratings were collected from the Fitch web page in November 2007. The approach taken is rather crude, as ratings collected in November 2007 were used for the data ranging from 2002 to 2007. CAM rating migrations were therefore not taken into account.

3.1. Doing so, it is assumed that all of the asset managers rated by Fitch Ratings are active on the CDO market. It can be seen that asset managers involved in structuring combination notes have an above average Fitch CAM rating. The effect is strong when averaging the asset manager rating by transaction, and only weak when averaging on an asset manager level (several asset managers appear more than once in the data). Taken together, these descriptive statistics indicate the importance of experience in structuring complex structures such as combination notes and can therefore be interpreted as support for hypothesis 6, which however can only be seen as a first step in its elaboration.

Rating information on the tranches is largely available in the dataset; the rating distribution can be found in table 3.2. Rating information was used in two ways: by using rating dummies and by generating numeric rating indices. Two indices have been generated, one without taking refinements into account, the *rating index*, and one with refinements, the *refined rating index*. For the rating index, AAA equals 10, AA equals 9, etc. For the refined rating index, AAA equals 22, AA+ equals 21, AA equals 20, etc. The entire mappings can be found in table 3.11 in the appendix. Ratings were collected from Standard & Poor's, Moody's, and Fitch. In case more than one rating was available and ratings differ, the index scores were averaged. However, split ratings were a minor problem, with 70 split ratings, thereof two split ratings for CNs and only two split ratings with a difference of two notches (A and AA-), all others having a difference of one on the refined index.[12] Here a further remark is necessary: as data is partly collected from pre-sale reports, some split ratings arise due to differences in preliminary ratings and are therefore not necessarily real split ratings.

Descriptive statistics on the deal level can be found in table 3.3. Deals are on average € 450 million in size, with 7.83 plain vanilla tranches (when combination notes are not taken into account), of which 4.85 are differently rated tranches (rating classes), and 2.98 are additional market classes. Rating classes

[12] Note that the rating index was derived from the refined rating index. Nine times the refined scores lie exactly between two rating grades (e.g. a score of 21.5 on the refined index). These were translated to the better rating grade on the rating index. Therefore, the rating index only takes on integer values.

Table 3.2: Rating distribution

Rating index	combination notes	plain vanilla tranches
5 (B)	3	6
6 (BB)	28	121
7 (BBB)	168	151
8 (A)	71	148
9 (AA)	31	146
10 (AAA)	57	284
not available	40	131
Nb tranches	398	987

and market classes were derived based on the refined rating index. Non-rated tranches were considered to be market classes. The mean of non-rated tranches is 1.04, with only four of the 131 non-rated tranches not being equity pieces. Thus, roughly speaking, by counting non-rated tranches as market classes the number of market classes per deal increases by one.

Additional variables were generated from the basic deal characteristics, such as an average rating score for the combination notes per deal, weighted average rating factors per deal, and a quarter index. The *average combination note rating* per deal is the value weighted average of the combination notes' rating using the rating index. However, when at least one CN rating is missing in a deal, the average CN rating is not calculated, as an average of the remaining CN ratings must not necessarily be a good proxy for all CN ratings in a deal. All CN ratings per deal and therefore the average CN rating are available for 98 deals.[13] The weighted average rating factor (WARF) per deal is based on rating factors published by Moody's and is used as a proxy for the quality of the underlying assets. While the WARF published by Moody's relies on the individual loans of the underlying asset pool, the WARF derived here relies on the ratings of the tranches of each deal, as more detailed information on the

[13] To make this more clear, consider a deal having three combination notes of equal size, two of them being rated AA, the third being unrated. When not considering the non-rated CN, the average CN rating for that deal would be nine, however, the non-rated CN could be of BB-quality, so the average CN rating should amount to eight. Therefore, the average CN rating is only calculated when a rating is available for all CNs in a deal.

Table 3.3: Descriptive statistics on the deal level – ex CN denotes variables that were generated without taking combination notes into account. Deal volume is in € millions. Rating classes and market classes are defined according to Firla-Cuchra / Jenkinson (2005). Share of deal FLP is the size of the FLP divided by the overall deal volume. Size CN is the aggregate volume of all combination notes in a deal in € millions. Share of deal CN is size CN divided by the deal volume. Tranche volume CN is the size of a single combination note in € millions. Equity fraction of CN is the equity share in one CN. Deal equity transferred is the share of deal equity transferred with one CN. The number of observations N is 126, except for the last three lines, where N is reported with each variable.

Variable	Mean	Std. Dev.	Min	Max
Deal volume (€ mio)	448.92	149.46	199.95	1000.00
Nb tranches ex CN	7.83	2.00	2.00	20.00
Nb rating classes ex CN	4.85	0.79	1.00	6.00
Nb market classes ex CN	2.98	1.86	0.00	16.00
Nb tranches not rated ex CN	1.04	0.43	0.00	4.00
Share of deal FLP (%)	0.09	0.03	0.005	0.26
Nb CN	3.16	2.05	1.00	9.00
Size CN (€ mio)	26.28	19.55	1.00	94.19
Share of deal CN (%)	0.06	0.05	0.002	0.24
Tranche volume CN (€ mio) (N=398)	8.32	6.69	1.00	69.00
Equity fraction of CN (%) (N=56)	0.26	0.19	0.00	0.75
Deal equity transferred (%) (N=56)	0.08	0.12	0.00	0.70

underlying assets is not available. The rating factors provided by Moody's are derived from idealized default probabilities that depend on ratings and maturities.[14] I use rating factors for ten year maturities (tabulated in table 3.11 in the appendix) and calculate the value weighted average of the tranches' rating factors for each deal, without taking the combination notes into account. The unrated first loss positions are treated as if they were rated CCC, as the lowest rated tranche in the dataset is rated B. As the relationship of ratings to the rating factors is non-linear, lower-rated securities have a stronger impact on the WARF, which results in a better differentiation of the WARF compared to using a measure such as the average rating. In the empirical analysis, the WARF is rescaled by taking the natural logarithm, which results in *lnWARF* as a proxy

[14] A tabulation of the idealized default probabilities can for example be found in Moody's (2003), p. 19. Rating factors are derived by dividing the default probabilities by the default probability of an Aaa-rated security of the same maturity. A rating factor of 80 indicates that the probability of default is 80 times higher than the probability of default for an Aaa-rated security with equal maturity.

for the quality of the underlying asset pool.[15] A higher lnWARF indicates lower asset pool quality. The *quarter index* is a variable that captures the time structure of the dataset. It is set to one for the quarter of the first observation in the data (July 2002), increases by one each quarter, and ends at 21 for the quarter of the last observation in the data (September 2007).

3.3.2 Exploring the properties of combination notes

The number of combination notes issued per deal is 3.16 on average, and the (aggregate) volume issued via combination notes per deal is € 26.28 million on average. A single combination note has an average volume of € 8.32 million, combination notes account for an average of 6% of the deal volume. Ratings on CNs differ and can address a rated balance that can differ from the principal balance; further ratings can address timely payment of interest and principal, ultimate payment of interest and principal, or ultimate payment of principal only.[16] Rating information is largely available on combination notes, as can be seen from table 3.2. Interestingly, only 31 combination notes are rated below investment grade, while the majority of CNs (60%) are rated either BBB or A. The rating distribution of CNs can be seen as a first indicator that CNs are tailored to specific investor needs, as a significant share of investors are likely to be obliged to hold only investment grade securities, be it due to internal or external constraints. Given that an investor is liable to bank regulation, CNs will likely have required a risk weight of 100% under Basel I, which might have implied regulatory capital arbitrage. Under Basel II, the treatment of CNs depends on the specific structural features of each CN.

For 56 combination notes that belong to 25 different deals, data on the actual note composition could be gathered. For theses 56 CNs the average share of equity comprised in one CN is 26%, and the average fraction of deal equity transferred with one CN is 8%. Taking this last number, roughly 25% of each deal's equity was transferred, which results in an estimate for the overall equity

[15] Equally, the WARF could be retranslated into a rating using table 3.11, though taking the natural logarithm makes better use of the available information.

[16] For the rating agencies' approaches see Standard & Poor's (2004), Moody's Investors Service (2004), and Fitch Ratings (2007).

transfer of € 1.24 billion for the 126 deals (3.16 CNs per deal × 8% of deal equity per CN × € 4.9 billion in overall equity).

Interestingly, 12 out of these 56 combination notes did not contain any equity and three times no equity was transferred via combination notes on the deal level at all. These three deals all comprised only one CN, two of them with a mix of A and BBB-rated tranches, and one with a mix of BBB and BB-rated tranches. Especially the creation of the two CNs composed of shares of A and BBB-rated tranches is puzzling, as not even a non-investment grade security is transformed to investment grade—as is the case for the CN composed of BBB and BB-rated tranches—as all of these 12 combination notes were at least rated investment grade. Most combination notes (47) were composed of parts of two tranches, whereas five CNs were composed of parts of three tranches, two CNs of parts of four and a further two of parts of five tranches.

For all 56 of these combination notes the rating is available. This rating is compared with a manually generated rating, the *CN rating revisited.* The CN rating revisited is the value weighted average of the CN components' ratings, based on the refined rating index.[17] In figure 3.1 the CN rating revisited is plotted against the true combination note rating. It can be seen that the actual rating for most combination notes is better than the manually calculated rating. Furthermore, none of the points lie substantially above the main diagonal. The dots are additionally distinguished by the type of rating that is shown on the x-axis. Circles represent ratings that are assigned to the ultimate repayment of principal only, whereas triangles represent ratings that are assigned to the ultimate payment of principal and a rated coupon. Consistently, the ratings that include the coupon are closer to the main diagonal, hence they are not substantially better than the manually derived CN rating revisited. Overall, this can be seen as another indication that combination notes are tailored to specific investor needs.

[17] A value of five is assigned to the FLP on the refined index, as the lowest rating in the data is a single B, which corresponds to eight on the refined rating index, and the FLP is considered being one entire notch down the rating scale. To take an example, a CN that consists of 30% AA, 30% BBB, and 40% equity is assigned a CN rating revisited of $0.3\times20+0.3\times14+0.4\times5=12.2$.

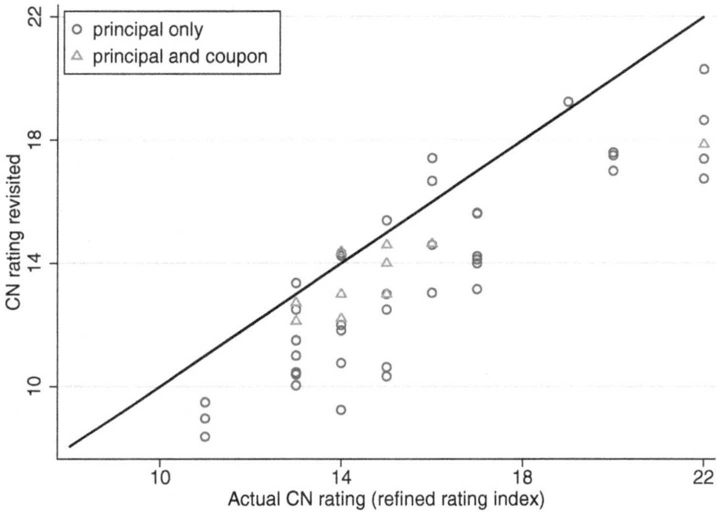

Figure 3.1: Actual rating CN vs. CN rating revisited

For 52 combination notes, launch spreads are available, as well.[18] However, these spreads must be treated carefully: from the data it is not possible to identify whether investors who hold these notes have a residual claim in addition to the spreads that appear in the data. As most of the combination notes comprise some equity, most CNs should comprise an upside potential even when a spread of a certain level is indicated. As launch spreads on combination notes are too few and not obvious to interpret they are not used in the further analysis.

3.4 Empirical analysis of combination notes

3.4.1 Determinants for the tranching of combination notes

The tranching decision was analyzed in depth by Firla-Cuchra / Jenkinson (2005), denoted C/J henceforth. They analyze three main determinants of tranching: investor sophistication, market segmentation, and asymmetric in-

[18] Launch spreads are measured in basis points and denote the spread over the corresponding benchmark, which is usually the six-month Euribor for the tranches considered here.

formation. Their main lines of thought are recapitulated in the context of this research in the following. C/J hypothesize and confirm that tranching is increasing in investor sophistication. For the data used here, investor sophistication is unlikely to be an important fact, as the data spans a rather recent period, while C/J use data ranging from 1987-2003. However, the quarter index is included in the following analysis to control for possible effects due to sophistication of market participants.

Given that market segmentation exists, there should be more tranching. A higher level of tranching can attract a larger investor base and reduce negative price effects on large tranches. However, tranching is costly in two ways: first, tranching has operative costs, for example legal costs and fees being due to rating agencies. Second, tranching can also be costly in terms of post-issue liquidity, as small tranches might not be marketable on secondary markets. C/J use the deal size to proxy for these effects of market segmentation. Large deals should be tranched more to be marketable on the primary market, while small deals should be tranched less to keep costs down and to maintain post-issue liquidity. This relation is confirmed by C/J, with a stronger impact of the deal volume on the number of market classes, and expected to hold here as well. However, contrary to C/J, I believe that the lower degree of tranching of small deals is associated rather with primary market activities, not post-issue liquidity on secondary markets: in case tranches become too small, marketing (from the originator's perspective) and research (from an investor's perspective) are not cost-efficient. The natural logarithm of the deal size (in millions) will be included in the analysis to control for these effects.[19]

Concerning information asymmetries, C/J hypothesize that a higher degree of asymmetric information should be associated with a larger number of tranches, especially of differently rated tranches. A higher number of rating classes releases more information on the underlying pool quality and therefore reduces information asymmetries. C/J construct an index that proxies the degree of information asymmetries by ranking the different types of underlying asset classes

[19] All the natural logarithms on tranche and deal volumes are taken on the values in millions, i.e. for a deal of size € 100 million Ln deal volume equals Ln(100).

according to their variability of launch spreads. Franke / Weber (2007) assume that information asymmetries are higher for CLO transactions than for CBOs and use a CLO dummy as a proxy variable for information asymmetries. As only very few transactions are classified as CLOs in the sense of Franke and Weber in this data, I instead use a leverage loan dummy, which is one in case the underlying assets are leveraged loans. For the leveraged loan dummy an argument similar to that for a CLO dummy can be made: information on leveraged loans underlying a securitization transaction are likely to be more difficult to obtain than information on publicly traded bonds or on tranches of CLOs and CDOs, the two other important types of underlying in the dataset. Comparing the volatility of launch spreads of the leveraged loan transactions to the volatility of launch spreads of the remainder of the dataset reveals that the volatility is higher among the leveraged loan securitizations. The volatility of launch spreads is calculated as the mean of the volatilities of launch spreads calculated per full letter rating grade. Furthermore, the ordering is not sensitive to the choice of a value weighted or equally weighted mean across the rating grades. Hence, the leveraged loan dummy is consistent with both the approach chosen by C/J and by Franke / Weber. Additionally, a level-management dummy is used as an alternative proxy for information problems. The level-management dummy is one in case the deal is fully managed. For fully managed transactions, information problems tend to be more pronounced due to hidden action problems.

Several control variables are employed by C/J, such as the quality of the underlying asset pool, actual bond market conditions, and WALs on the deal level (value weighted averages of tranche WALs). The impact of the asset pool quality is ambiguous. While C/J hypothesize a positive relationship for the pool quality and the number of rating classes, a negative relationship is assumed by Franke / Weber (2007). Both C/J and Franke / Weber find some, but limited support for their hypotheses. In chapter 4, based on a transactions cost-driven hypothesis, I find support for an increasing number of rating classes given a decrease in asset pool quality. Concerning the actual bond market conditions, C/J argue that severe bond market conditions require a more pronounced catering to investor needs and hence imply a higher number of market classes. C/J find that for a steep yield curve less rating classes and more market classes are issued. In the following, the lnWARF will be used to control for deal quality, while bond market conditions are captured by using the yield of ten year AAA Euroland government bonds provided by Datastream and the difference between ten year and two year AAA Euroland government bond yields. As the average WAL is available only for a subset of the data, it is not used in the following specifications, but results are robust to adding the average WAL.

Subsequently, three tranching decisions will be analyzed. First, tranching is analyzed without taking the combination notes into account, which serves as a reference case to C/J and to the further analysis. Thereafter, tranching within the combination notes and the tranching of combination notes in the deal context will be analyzed. The tranching decision within the combination notes of a deal can provide evidence on market segmentation, while the tranching decision of combination notes in the deal context might shed light on the reduction of information asymmetries. The tranching decision is analyzed by running ordered logistic regressions. Some of the analyzed numbers of tranches are unequally distributed at the lower and the higher end. In that case, numbers of tranches below the 10% and above the 90% quantiles of the data are grouped together at the 10% or 90% quantiles of the relevant number of tranches. Further, the subsequently presented regressions do not violate the parallel regression assumption inherent to ordered logistic regression. As a further robustness test, Poisson regressions have been run, with the major results being unchanged.

3.4.1.1 The benchmark case – tranching of plain vanilla tranches

The analysis of tranching without taking the combination notes into account should reveal results similar to C/J. However, models on the overall number of tranches and the number of market classes are not of statistical significance, which is probably due to the small sample size (126 deals compared to 1605 in C/J). Therefore, only the regression of the number of rating classes on all of the explanatory variables lined out above is reported in table 3.4. Only the leveraged loan dummy and the slope of the yield curve turn out statistically significant at

Table 3.4: Tranching of plain vanilla tranches – The dependent variable is the number of rating classes without taking combination notes into account. Results are reported for ordered logit estimation. Heteroscedasticity-robust standard errors are reported in parentheses. Significance of coefficients is indicated by asterisks, where ***, **, and * denote significance at the 1%, 5%, and 10% level, respectively.

Ln deal volume	LL dummy	lnWARF	Quarter index	Yield level	Yield slope
0.261	1.721**	0.135	-0.076	0.121	-2.313**
(0.613)	(0.671)	(0.345)	(0.101)	(0.459)	(0.929)
Sample size: 126		McFadden's R^2: 0.171		Prob > χ^2: 0.000	

the 5% level. The coefficient on the leveraged loan dummy, given that it proxies for information asymmetries, shows the expected sign. When it is replaced by the fully-managed dummy, the coefficient on the fully-managed dummy is positive as well, but not statistically significant, while the coefficient on the lnWARF increases in size and turns statistically significant at the 1% level (not reported). Thus, the LL dummy could also proxy for a lower asset pool quality that is not captured in the lnWARF, and is associated with a higher degree of tranching; see also chapter 4. Hence, there is some but limited evidence that information asymmetries drive the creation of differently rated tranches, just as there is some but limited evidence that the number of differently rated tranches rises with decreasing quality of the underlying asset pool. Consistent with C/J, the deal volume does not have a strong impact on the number of differently rated tranches. Further, increasing investor sophistication, proxied by the quarter index, does not have an impact in this comparably short time period. Again in line with C/J, the slope of the yield curve has a negative impact on the number of rating classes. As will be shown below, higher long-term interest rates have an increasing effect on launch spreads, and hence make securitization more expensive. An increase in the slope of the yield curve thus can prevent the creation of tranches, likely at the bottom of a securitization structure, as these tranches become increasingly expensive to issue.

3.4.1.2 Tranching of combination notes

In this section, tranching within the combination notes is analyzed. For this purpose, the number of rating classes and market classes have been derived when *only* considering combination notes of each deal.[20] There are several non-rated combination notes. Non-rated CNs are considered market classes, which is consistent with the approach taken for the plain vanilla tranches. However, counting non-rated CNs as market classes could introduce a bias, as some of the non-rated CNs may actually be rated but the rating is not available in the dataset. Therefore, the number of market classes was additionally derived without considering the non-rated tranches as market classes, but results remain unchanged (not reported). In nine deals not a single CN is rated. These deals are dropped for the further analysis of rating and market classes, which results in 117 observations. On average, there are 2.39 rating classes and 0.85 market classes amongst the combination notes per deal, when non-rated tranches are considered market classes.[21] Again, ordered logit is estimated and regressions are run for the overall number of tranches, the number of rating classes and the number of market classes. The lnWARF is not considered to be an explanatory variable in this setting as a reasonable link between the underlying asset pool quality and the tranching decision within CNs cannot be established.

As stated in hypothesis 1, the number of combination notes is expected to rise with the absolute volume of combination notes in a deal. This relation should hold for the number of rating and market classes, but be stronger for the number of market classes, given that there exists a negative relation for the size of a CN and its marketability. The data strongly supports this hypothesis, as can be seen from table 3.5. The coefficients on the aggregate CN volume (Ln size CN) are highly significant and of the expected sign for all the different dependent variables, and the coefficient is larger for market classes than for rating classes. Predicted probabilities show that for small aggregate CN volumes the probabil-

[20] To take an example, a deal that comprises three combination notes, one rated AA and two rated A, comprises two rating classes and one market class among the combination notes, independently of the rating and number of plain vanilla tranches in the deal.

[21] The average number of combination notes in these 117 deals lies at 3.25, hence slightly above the average number of combination notes in the whole dataset as reported in table 3.3.

Table 3.5: Tranching of combination notes – The dependent variables are the number of combination notes per deal, the number of rating classes within the combination notes, and the number of market classes within the combination notes where not rated combination notes are considered being market classes. Results are reported for ordered logit estimation. Heteroscedasticity-robust standard errors are reported in parentheses next to the coefficients. Significance of coefficients is indicated by asterisks, where ***, **, and * denote significance at the 1%, 5%, and 10% level, respectively.

Dependent var.	all		rating		market	
Ln size CN	3.468***	(0.433)	2.366***	(0.355)	2.923***	(0.537)
LL dummy	0.815*	(0.443)	1.058**	(0.475)	−0.155	(0.530)
Quarter index	0.068	(0.156)	−0.003	(0.219)	−0.003	(0.202)
Yield level	−1.305*	(0.729)	−1.545*	(0.907)	0.454	(0.675)
Yield slope	0.639	(1.282)	−0.236	(1.620)	0.965	(1.446)
Sample size	126		117		117	
McFadden's R^2	0.347		0.291		0.361	
Prob > χ^2	0.000		0.000		0.000	

ity for only a single combination note and hence for a single rating class is very high, while in this case, obviously, a very high probability is assigned to zero market classes. Probabilities for higher numbers of rating and market classes rise with rising aggregate combination note volumes. For a more detailed understanding, table 3.6 presents predicted probabilities for the number of rating classes among the combination notes for several discrete values of Ln size CN.

As reported above, the leveraged loan dummy is associated with a higher number of plain vanilla rating classes. This must not hold for the tranching within combination notes for two reasons. First, combination notes are a combination of plain vanilla tranches and should therefore not reveal additional information on the underlying loss distribution. Second, the rating classes considered here are not necessarily unique ratings in the deal, as only the tranching within the CNs is considered. However, the coefficient on the LL dummy is positive and significant for the overall number of CNs and for the number of rating classes among the CNs. A possible explanation is that a higher degree of tranching on the level of plain vanilla tranches is associated with a higher degree of tranching of CNs, which will also be supported in the next section. Another explanation might be that the average quality of the underlying assets in leveraged loan securitization is below the quality of the remaining transactions in the

Table 3.6: Predicted probabilities for discrete changes in Ln size CN – The table presents predicted probabilities for the number of ratings classes within the combination notes for several values of Ln size CN. All other variables of the model (model 2 in table 3.5) are held at their mean. The mean of size CN is at € 26.28 million, Ln(26.28) ≈ 3.27.

	$x=1$	$x=2$	$x=3$	$x=4$	$x=4.5$
$P(y=1 \mid x)$	0.9678	0.7382	0.2093	0.0242	0.0076
$P(y=2 \mid x)$	0.0270	0.2089	0.4175	0.1119	0.0385
$P(y=3 \mid x)$	0.0044	0.0438	0.2838	0.3524	0.1803
$P(y=4 \mid x)$	0.0009	0.0091	0.0895	0.5115	0.7736

data, and lower quality assets are only marketable in smaller tranches. Adding the lnWARF to the model removes the significance from the LL dummy for the second model (rating classes), while the coefficient on the lnWARF is positive and significant at the 10% level (not reported). The other two models are not substantially altered by adding the lnWARF. Investor sophistication, proxied by the quarter index, did not help to explain tranching in the section above. For combination notes, an increasing number of combination notes could be expected with the quarter index, as the market for combination notes might not have been as mature in 2002 as the securitization market in general, which however is not supported by the data. Again, the interest rate environment is controlled for by using the slope and the level of the yield curve. Consistent with the results derived on plain vanilla tranching, the level of long-term yields has a negative, statistically weak, impact on the number of all CNs and the number of rating classes.

Overall, the aggregated size of the combination notes in a deal strongly determines their tranching. For univariate regressions of the different dependent variables on the ln size CN variable, pseudo R^2s take the values of 32.9%, 25.4%, and 33.2%.

3.4.1.3 Tranching of combination notes versus the deal

In this last subsection on tranching, the tranching of combination notes is analyzed in the context of the existing deal structure. Again, rating and market classes are derived. Now, the number of rating classes amongst the combination notes is the number of *newly created* ratings when comparing the combination notes to the plain vanilla tranches of the deal (hence *versus* the plain vanilla deal structure). The remainder of the combination notes is classified as market classes.[22] Using this definition, the average number of rating classes among the CNs decreases to 1.2, while the average number of market classes increases to 2.05. Ordered logit is estimated for two specifications, which are discussed in the following. In the first model specification, only the variables that were used when analyzing plain vanilla tranching are considered as explanatory variables. Using this first model, the impact of general deal characteristics on the tranching of combination notes versus the deal is analyzed. Model two controls for CN characteristics. The number of observations drops to 98 for the second specification as the average combination note rating is only available for that subset of the data.

For the first specification, the most interesting variable is the LL dummy. By structuring combination notes, it is possible to add new ratings to an existing securitization structure, captured as rating classes in this section. This new rating could possibly add additional information on the underlying asset pool and therefore reduce information asymmetries, as stated in hypothesis 3. The data does not support this hypothesis: there is evidence that more CNs overall and more market classes are issued for LL transactions in specification one, but there is no impact of the LL dummy on the number of rating classes. The positive effect on the number of market classes can be explained by endogeneity rather than by economic reasoning: given that more plain vanilla rating classes are created for LL transactions as denoted in section 3.4.1.1, there are less 'free' rating notches available to be filled by combination notes. Replacing the LL dummy by the fully-managed dummy (not reported) also does not indicate that CNs are structured to mitigate agency conflicts. Therefore, hypothesis 3 must be rejected. The three other additional general deal characteristics, i.e. the

[22] To take an example: a deal that comprises one AAA, two AA+, one A, one BBB and one non-rated FLP and additionally three combination notes, two of them rated AA-, one rated A, comprises one rating class and two market classes amongst the combination notes versus the deal, as one new rating is generated in the overall deal structure (AA-).

Table 3.7: Tranching of combination notes versus the deal – The dependent variables are the number of combination notes per deal, the number of rating classes of CNs versus the deal, and the number of market classes of CNs versus the deal. Results are reported for ordered logit estimation. Heteroscedasticity-robust standard errors are reported in parentheses below the coefficients. Significance of coefficients is indicated by asterisks, where ***, **, and * denote significance at the 1%, 5%, and 10% level, respectively.

	I			II		
Dependent var.	all	rating	market	all	rating	market
Ln deal volume	0.809	0.093	1.038	0.077	−0.683	0.840
	(0.687)	(0.797)	(0.643)	(1.268)	(0.978)	(0.861)
LL dummy	0.873**	0.277	1.170**	0.505	0.073	0.867
	(0.423)	(0.507)	(0.557)	(0.788)	(0.656)	(0.795)
lnWARF	0.170	0.610	−0.074	0.487	0.928	−0.787
	(0.209)	(0.385)	(0.283)	(1.007)	(0.582)	(0.904)
Quarter index	0.160	0.017	0.097	−0.085	0.012	0.086
	(0.121)	(0.145)	(0.098)	(0.173)	(0.154)	(0.175)
Yield level	−1.494***	−1.075*	−0.654*	−0.355	−0.125	−0.172
	(0.455)	(0.574)	(0.395)	(1.118)	(0.695)	(0.722)
Yield slope	2.025**	0.562	1.715**	−0.091	0.253	1.481
	(0.922)	(1.091)	(0.742)	(1.558)	(1.153)	(1.342)
Ln size CN				3.390***	1.120***	2.204***
				(0.494)	(0.368)	(0.422)
Nb rating cl. ex CN				0.537**	0.385	0.399
				(0.268)	(0.249)	(0.300)
Average rating CN				−0.123	−1.021***	0.616**
				(0.269)	(0.294)	(0.271)
Sample size	126	117	117	98	98	98
McFadden's R^2	0.056	0.043	0.054	0.354	0.146	0.278
Prob > χ^2	0.001	0.023	0.001	0.000	0.005	0.000

deal volume, the quarter index, and the lnWARF, do not have an impact on the tranching decision of CNs versus the deal. When looking at the interest rate environment, results are mixed and opposed to the results derived above. However, pseudo R^2s are comparably low for all dependent variables for the first model specification, and adding the CN specific information in the second model specification removes all statistical significance from the coefficients of the first model.

In the second specification the regressions controll for the aggregate CN volume, the average rating of the combination notes, and the number of rating classes among the plain vanilla tranches. The pseudo R^2 rises sharply, and all three variables have strong explanatory power. The size of the aggregate CN volume again is the dominating variable. The average combination note rating is endogenous in nature, but still helpful. As indicated by the coefficients, a high average CN rating implies less rating and more market classes among the CNs versus the plain vanilla tranches. Given that the rating distribution for the plain vanilla tranches is skewed towards high rating grades (more than 50% of all plain vanilla tranches are rated AA- or better, and 32% are rated AAA), it is by definition less likely that a new rating class is generated when the rating assigned to the CN is high. New ratings are more likely to arise for lower-rated combination notes. The number of rating classes among the plain vanilla tranches is also endogenous in nature: given a high number of rating classes among the plain vanilla tranches, the likelihood for creating a new rating class by a CN should fall. For the overall number of CNs, a positive relation can be observed with the number of rating classes among the plain vanilla tranches. Hence, sophisticated structuring of the deal is associated with the creation of more CNs. Surprisingly, the number of rating classes of the CNs versus the deal does not decreases with a rising number of rating classes among the plain vanilla tranches. Apparently the effect of a rising number of CNs outweighs the endogeneity of a higher number of rating classes among the plain vanilla tranches (fewer gaps to fill).

Summarizing the results, combination notes seem not to be structured to solve information asymmetries; hypothesis 3 can be rejected. Meanwhile, strong support is found for hypothesis 1: tranching of combination notes is almost entirely driven by segmentation effects. This result suggests that combination notes are only marketable below a certain size and implies a fairly constant absolute size of combination notes. As noted above, the average volume of a single CN is € 8.32 million, with a standard deviation of only € 6.69 million, a minimum value of € 1 million, a maximum of € 69 million, and the 95%-percentile at € 20 million. Additionally, the more sophisticated the original structuring of the deal, the higher the number of CNs. New rating classes versus the deal arise mainly at low ratings. There is no evidence that CNs are specifically tailored to fill rating gaps among the plain vanilla rating classes.

3.4.2 Combination notes and risk transfer

3.4.2.1 Measuring equity transfer

It was shown above that CNs are mainly structured to cater to segmented demand, but not to transmit additional information on the underlying asset pool by their tranching. From an originator's perspective, combination notes mainly are a means to repackage and transfer equity. As noted above, for a subset of the data the exact composition of combination notes is available, with an average deal equity transfer of 8% by each single CN. To be able to test hypotheses concerning the equity transfer via combination notes such as H2, H4, and H5 for the entire dataset, a risk or equity transfer proxy is necessary. Two variables capture the amount of equity transfer: the relative size of the aggregate combination note volume per deal, and the average rating of the combination notes per deal. As laid out in section 3.3.2 the average equity fraction per single CN is 26%, with a standard deviation of 19% for the subset of 56 CNs. Further, the equity fraction of the single CNs is found to be independent of the size of the relevant CNs. Hence, given a comparably constant relative equity fraction per combination note, the share of equity transferred on a deal level will rise with the relative CN volume in a deal. Testing this relation on the 19 deals where the exact CN composition is known for all CNs, it is strongly supported: the fraction of deal equity transferred rises in the relative size of the CNs of the deal.[23] Hence, even though there is variation in the equity fraction per CN, a larger relative CN volume strongly indicates that more equity is transferred to the market. Therefore, the relative size of the aggregate CN volume per deal can serve as a measure of equity transfer, and is called *share of deal CN*. The variation in the equity fraction per CN could be captured in each CN's rating, with a larger equity fraction implying a lower rating. This information was captured in a former version of this article to derive an equity transfer proxy that equalled the share of deal CN divided by the average combination note rating of the relevant deal. The proxy variable showed similar but slightly weaker results

[23] A univariate OLS regression of the fraction of deal equity transferred onto the relative size of the CNs results in a highly significant coefficient of about four for the relative size of the CNs, and a R^2 of about 76%.

to when using the share of deal CN variable on a stand-alone basis. This can be due to a reduction in the sample size but also to the ambiguity concerning the meaning of combination note ratings (rating to a rated balance, principal-only ratings, etc.). Subsequently, results are only reported for the share of deal CN variable.

3.4.2.2 Equity transfer and deal characteristics

Hypotheses 2 and 4 both make a prediction about the relative size of the combination notes in a deal. H2 states that the relative size of the CNs in a deal will decrease with the volume of the deal due to a limited market capacity for the equity of a single transaction. H2 can hence provide further support for the idea of segmented markets. H4 states that, as it is not possible to arbitrarily increase the amount of equity in a single CN, the relative CN volume will rise for lower deal quality, assuming that risk transfer is a transaction motive. Support for this hypothesis would indicate that CNs are indeed structured as equity transfer vehicles.

To test these hypotheses, two ordinary least squares regressions are run with the share of deal CN as the dependent variable. The explanatory variables of most interest are the deal volume (used in logarithmic form) and lnWARF as a proxy for the quality of the underlying assets, which are tested on a stand-alone basis in model I. Several control variables are added in model II. The time structure is captured by the quarter index. Proceeding in time could have different implications for the amount of equity transfer: investors might be more familiar with CNs and be willing to buy larger CNs, or CNs that comprise more equity. Contrarily, as equity pieces are being sold more often directly in recent years, the issuance of CNs might become less important to originators. The number of rating classes among the plain vanilla tranches should have a positive impact on the equity transfer, because a higher number of plain vanilla rating classes is associated with a higher number of CNs. The level and slope of the yield curve again are used to control for market conditions. Given the pure expectations theory, a steep yield curve is associated with rising interest rates, and hence less favorable future market conditions from the originator's perspective. More

Table 3.8: Equity transfer and deal characteristics – The dependent variable is share of deal CN. OLS is estimated. Heteroscedasticity-robust standard errors are reported in parentheses next to the coefficients. Significance of coefficients is indicated by asterisks, where ***, **, and * denote significance at the 1%, 5%, and 10% level, respectively.

	I		II	
lnWARF	0.010***	(0.004)	0.008*	(0.004)
Ln deal volume	−0.025**	(0.012)	−0.022*	(0.012)
Quarter index			0.004*	(0.002)
Nb rating cl. ex CN			0.018***	(0.005)
Yield level			−0.019*	(0.011)
Yield slope			0.060***	(0.017)
Constant	0.149*	(0.082)	0.044	(0.094)
Sample size	126		126	
Adjusted R^2	0.037		0.181	
Prob > F	0.001		0.000	

generally, a steep yield curve should be related to an overall favorable macroeconomic environment and might facilitate equity transfer due to low levels of risk aversion. A steep yield curve should hence be associated with high selling activities, and therefore also with a higher degree of risk transfer. The leveraged loan dummy is not considered to be a control variable, as, from a risk transfer perspective, there should not be a difference in the specific type of underlying.[24]

Table 3.8 presents the results, which support H2 as well as H4. Concerning H2, coefficients on the deal volume are of the expected sign and significant at 5% and 10%. Estimates in model I indicate that an increase of 10% in the deal size roughly reduces the share of deal CN by about 0.0025 in absolute terms (the mean value for the share of deal CN is at 0.06). Hence, the market for combination notes of a single deal and therefore equity seems to be bound from above. Concerning H4, estimates in model I indicate that an increase of the lnWARF by one induces an increase of the share of deal CN of 0.01. An increase of the lnWARF by one would, to take an example, roughly correspond to a move from an average A-rated asset pool to an average BBB-rated asset

[24] The LL dummy turns out not significant when added to the analysis, but removes explanatory power from the lnWARF variable. This again indicates a lower quality of leveraged loan transactions.

pool. This positive and statistically significant relation indicates that CNs are used as risk transfer vehicles by their originators. The control variables add additional insights and remove some significance from the deal volume and the lnWARF. There is weak support that equity transfer increased during the sample period, which might be linked to rising investor sophistication. Coefficients for the number of plain vanilla rating classes and the slope of the yield curve are as expected and highly significant. The number of plain vanilla rating classes and the slope of the yield curve explain a substantial fraction of the variation: when only using these two variables as explanatory variables, adjusted R^2 reaches 13.6%. Dropping both the deal volume and lnWARF from model II reduces the adjusted R^2 to 15.8%.

Several robustness checks have been performed and are laid out in the following, but not reported. The lnWARF was replaced by the relative size of the FLP. The relative size of the FLP equally is a proxy for a lower deal quality, although it is not as comprehensive as the lnWARF. Coefficients on the relative size of the FLP are positive, in line with H4, but not statistically significant in most specifications. Equivalent regressions have been run on the subsample of 19 deals where the true CN compositions are available, with the volume of equity truly transferred via CNs as a share of the overall deal volume as the dependent variable. The signs of all coefficients remain unchanged, while coefficients in model I lose their significance, and the significance of coefficients in model II either remains at the levels reported in table 3.8 or increases. Further, given that the share of deal CN variable is a fractional dependent variable, a generalized linear model following Papke and Wooldridge (1996) was estimated, using a logit link and the binomial family. Results remain almost unchanged, though the significance of the coefficient on the deal amount increases to the 5% level in model II. Marginal effects evaluated at the means of the regressors are very close to the coefficients obtained using OLS. Overall, even though the control variables explain a substantial fraction of variation in the data, the coefficients on the deal amount and the lnWARF have the expected sign, are statistically significant, and are robust to alternative model specifications.

3.4.2.3 Equity transfer and launch spreads

Empirical literature on bond spreads grew substantially in recent years, with several articles focusing on corporate bonds.[25] Studies on the pricing of asset backed securities are still rare. Boudoukh et al. (1997) examine the pricing of MBS by the level and slope of the yield curve. Scheicher (2008) examines spread changes on CDS index tranches of the iTraxx and the CDX. Longstaff and Rajan (2008) decompose CDX spreads into three major components: idiosyncratic risk, sector default risk, and systemic risk. The two closest related studies to the analysis presented here are Firla-Cuchra (2005) and Firla-Cuchra / Jenkinson (2005) (C/J). Both focus on launch spreads of ABS in level form, just as the remainder of this section will do. Firla-Cuchra (2005) finds that launch spreads are well described by credit ratings without refinements, but variables associated with liquidity, market segmentation, distribution efforts, and the prevailing legal regime can explain further variation in launch spreads. C/J analyze the impact of tranching on the pricing of ABS. They find that a higher number of predicted rating classes reduces launch spreads, while it is controlled for all common pricing factors.

The purpose of this section is to examine whether the amount of observed equity transfer, proxied via combination note properties, has an impact on the pricing of plain vanilla securities, i.e. hypothesis 5 is tested. Combination notes are observed by market participants, and could be a positive signal to plain vanilla tranche investors: some other market participant is directing funds towards a share of the FLP, the most subordinate security of the deal that protects other investors. An investment in that security by a market participant could therefore be interpreted as quality signal for the deal in general, and imply lower launch spreads. Again, the share of deal CN variable is used to measure the equity transfer. Methodologically, the following analysis is equivalent to C/J and Firla-Cuchra (2005). The majority of the explanatory variables used in C/J and Firla-Cuchra (2005) are used in this study. The dependent variable

[25] See for example Duffee (1998), Elton et al. (2001), Collin-Dufresne / Goldstein / Martin (2001), Perraudin / Taylor (2003), Campbell / Taksler (2003), Driessen (2005), and Amato / Remolona (2005).

is the natural logarithm of launch spreads, with almost all launch spreads referring to Euribor. Combination notes, equity pieces, fixed rate issues, zero bonds, and super senior swaps are excluded from the analysis, which reduces the data to 766 floating rate notes. The origination spread is available on 718 of these floaters, belonging to 124 deals. Two different approaches are taken in the following. First, all launch spreads are analyzed in a pooled regression, and the tranche's rating is captured by rating dummies or the refined rating index. Second, tranches are organized according to their rating and launch spreads are analyzed within the different rating categories to derive a better understanding of pricing factors beyond ratings.

For the first approach, seven models are estimated with OLS, considering three groups of explanatory variables: credit rating information, interest rate parameters, and deal and tranche-specific information. Standard errors are heteroscedasticity-robust, and the estimation of standard errors accounts for the fact that tranches are not necessarily independent within a deal, but independent for different deals. Results are reported in table 3.9. Model I only uses rating dummies without refinements, with A being the omitted credit rating. Rating dummies were derived from the rating index, and as such are based on average ratings in case differing ratings from more than one agency were available. All coefficients are significant at 0.1%. Comparing the results to Firla-Cuchra (2005), R^2 is significantly higher, at about 90%, while Firla-Cuchra reports an R^2 of 71.9% when only controlling for rating.[26] This strong difference could be due to two reasons: the data used here is very homogeneous in types of underlying assets and the time period is comparably short; by contrast, data used by Firla-Cuchra spans over 16 years and is based on various underlyings. However, even when controlling for the time dimension and types of underlying, and also for deal characteristics and market conditions, R^2s reported by Firla-Cuchra and C/J are clearly below the 90% reached here. The reason for the high level of R^2 observed here might be that even within the category of collateralized debt obligations, the underlying is very homogeneous in the data with 97 leveraged loan deals out of 126 deals. Model II adds the share of deal CN variable. Given that

[26] See Firla-Cuchra (2005), p. 14, model III.

H5 holds, the sign on the coefficient should be negative, which is confirmed by the data. Still, the coefficient is not statistically significant and the R^2 remains unchanged.

The second set of controls are the level and slope of the yield curve, again measured by the ten year yield on AAA Euroland government bonds provided by Datastream and the difference in 10-2 year yields, both used on a weekly basis and in units of percentage points. Using this specification, the two year yield is also fully incorporated in the analysis, captured in the slope variable when holding the ten year yield fixed. Model III adds these two interest rate parameters to model I. R^2 rises by about 5%, coefficients are significant at 0.1%. The interpretation of coefficients needs to be done carefully. An absolute increase in the two year yield of ten basis points (i.e. a decrease in the slope while keeping the ten year yield fixed) leads to a reduction of launch spreads of about 3.8%. This is consistent with empirical findings by Duffee (1998) and with the contingent claims analysis on corporate bonds by Longstaff and Schwartz (1995). Conversely, an increase of ten basis points on the ten year yield is associated with launch spreads being about 6% higher, considering the coefficients on the level and the slope holding the two year yield fixed. These results on the long-term yield and the slope differ from existing evidence. The slope of the yield curve is rather expected to have a negative effect on credit spreads: a steep yield curve is associated with a sound economic climate, which implies comparably high recovery rates and thus lower credit spreads. Further, following the expectations theory, a steep yield curve is associated with rising future short rates, which should result in lower credit spreads due to the results obtained by Longstaff and Schwartz (1995).[27] This negative relation is confirmed by Duffee (1998), as he finds a negative coefficient for increases in long-term yields. Campbell and Taksler (2003) find only limited support with a changing sign for the coefficients on the slope. Collin-Dufresne / Goldstein / Martin (2001) find a strong negative relation between long-term interest rates and bond spreads, but only weak statistical significance for the slope coefficient. Scheicher (2008) finds mixed and comparably weak results concerning the impact of changes in

[27] See Collin-Dufresne / Goldstein / Martin (2001) for these arguments.

the level and the slope of the yield curve on changes of index tranche spreads. Coefficients are only significant for the level of the yield curve and only when it is controlled for the time period of the subprime crisis; furthermore, coefficients differ for the iTraxx and the CDX.

Firla-Cuchra's results also differ from the results obtained here. Firla-Cuchra uses the ten year yield and 10-2 year swap yields. In that specification, he finds a negative coefficient on the slope for most model specifications, indicating a positive impact of higher short-term interest on launch spreads. Looking at the level and slope together, Firla-Cuchra's results indicate a negative impact of higher long-term interest rates on launch spreads. Coefficients however are not significant when only focusing on CDOs.[28] Results from C/J are similar to those from Firla-Cuchra (2005).[29] Given the differences to my results concerning the level and the slope of the yield curve and its impact on launch spreads, I tested the relationship on a comprehensive dataset of CDO origination spreads containing over 3000 observations; results remain similar to the results presented in tables 3.9 and 3.10. These differences, especially to the findings by Firla-Cuchra, highlight the need for further research on the pricing of bundled credit risk on primary markets.

Reconsidering equity transfer and launch spreads, the share of deal CN variable is again added to the regression in model IV. The coefficient on the share of deal CN has the predicted negative sign and is significant at 0.1%. An increase in the relative aggregate CN volume in a deal by 0.01 implies a decrease of launch spreads of approximately 1.1%. The R^2, however, remains almost unchanged.

The last set of control variables are deal and tranche-specific information and are added in model V. In model V I additionally take into account the size of the deal a tranche belongs to and the size of each tranche itself. The deal and tranche size can possibly have two opposing impacts: while a large deal or tranche might be more difficult to market and hence more expensive to place in

[28] See Firla-Cuchra (2005), p. 20, table 5, model V.

[29] Firla-Cuchra and C/J additionally control for interest rate volatility to capture possible effects of the value of prepayment options on the launch spread. Prepayments are not an issue for the data on European CDOs used here; the interest rate volatility is thus not considered.

Table 3.9: Launch spreads and risk transfer (i) – The dependent variable in all regressions is the natural logarithm of each tranche's launch spread. OLS is estimated. Heteroscedasticity-robust standard errors are reported in parentheses, with the clustering of tranches within deals being taken into account. All regressions include a constant, which is not reported. Significance of coefficients is indicated as follows: bold coefficients are significant at 0.1%, bold and italic coefficients are significant at 1%, and coefficients with one asterisk are significant at 5%.

	I	II	III	IV	V	VI	VII
Dummy AAA	**-0.974**	**-0.974**	**-0.966**	**-0.964**	**-0.795**	**-0.783**	
	(0.022)	(0.022)	(0.017)	(0.017)	(0.040)	(0.039)	
Dummy AA	**-0.453**	**-0.453**	**-0.466**	**-0.466**	**-0.434**	**-0.430**	
	(0.033)	(0.033)	(0.023)	(0.022)	(0.019)	(0.018)	
Dummy BBB	**0.829**	**0.829**	**0.827**	**0.829**	**0.793**	**0.792**	
	(0.029)	(0.029)	(0.019)	(0.019)	(0.018)	(0.018)	
Dummy BB	**1.736**	**1.736**	**1.757**	**1.758**	**1.710**	**1.704**	
	(0.032)	(0.032)	(0.020)	(0.020)	(0.025)	(0.026)	
Dummy B	**1.925**	**1.925**	**2.078**	**2.092**	**1.999**	**1.990**	
	(0.054)	(0.054)	(0.073)	(0.064)	(0.055)	(0.053)	
Refined rating index							**-0.216**
							(0.003)
Yield level			**0.215**	**0.191**	**0.227**	**0.209**	**0.201**
			(0.048)	(0.045)	(0.038)	(0.035)	(0.037)
Yield slope			**0.384**	**0.410**	**0.350**	**0.381**	**0.400**
			(0.033)	(0.032)	(0.033)	(0.033)	(0.034)
Share of deal CN		-0.013		**-1.087**		***-1.049***	***-1.041***
		(0.538)		(0.303)		(0.321)	(0.323)

continued on next page

Table 3.9 continued

	I	II	III	IV	V	VI	VII
Ln deal volume					-0.003	-0.025	-0.029
					(0.048)	(0.045)	(0.045)
Ln tranche volume					**-0.074**	**-0.078**	**-0.054**
					(0.012)	(0.012)	(0.010)
Share of deal FLP					0.859	0.919	0.283
					(0.788)	(0.771)	(0.789)
Credit enhancement					-0.270*	***-0.289***	-0.015
					(0.114)	(0.110)	(0.098)
Nb rating classes ex CN					-0.008	0.014	0.005
					(0.022)	(0.024)	(0.024)
LL dummy					***-0.177***	***-0.168***	***-0.155***
					(0.054)	(0.052)	(0.055)
Sample size	718	718	718	718	718	718	718
Adjusted R^2	0.899	0.899	0.952	0.955	0.962	0.964	0.948
Prob > F	0.000	0.000	0.000	0.000	0.000	0.000	0.000
Clusters	124	124	124	124	124	124	124

segmented markets, the liquidity of large deals or tranches on secondary markets will be greater. Firla-Cuchra (2005) finds a negative coefficient on the overall deal volume but a positive coefficient on the tranche size, which indicates that, on a tranche level, there is a negative effect of demand on price (i.e. higher launch spreads), whereas on the deal level the liquidity effect is dominant.[30] Results found here indicate that the liquidity effect dominates on the tranche level as well, as all coefficients are highly significant and of negative sign. Coefficients on the deal size are negative, as well, but not significant in any specification.

Furthermore, model V accounts for the share of the FLP on the deal, the level of credit enhancements, the number of plain vanilla rating classes, and the leveraged loan dummy. The share of the FLP on the overall deal volume could have a similar impact as the share of the CNs on the deal volume: a larger first loss position allows more defaults to happen until a plain vanilla tranche is hit. However, as the credit ratings basically arise from the structuring process and thus also from the size of the FLP, the variable is not expected to have explanatory power, which is confirmed by the data.

There are various possibilities for credit enhancements in securitization transactions.[31] The credit enhancement captured here is the fraction of the deal subordinated to the relevant tranche of interest. Information captured in the credit enhancement is closely related to the rank in the deal of the relevant tranche, therefore only the credit enhancement is used. The credit enhancement captures additional information that is not captured in the credit rating, as even within a rating category enhancement levels can differ according to the rank in deal. A negative coefficient is expected as a higher enhancement level indicates higher protection in case of defaults in the underlying asset pool. Credit enhancement is significant on 5% and 1% in models V and VI and of the expected sign.

C/J show that the number of rating classes has a negative impact on launch spreads. While they predict the number of rating classes from an ordered logit model on the number of rating classes, the actual number of rating classes is

[30] See Firla-Cuchra (2005), p. 23, table 6.

[31] See Hein (2006) for a simulation-based analysis of internal credit enhancements.

used here. The findings of C/J are not supported by the dataset used here, which is also robust to using the predicted number of rating classes (not reported).

Finally, the LL dummy is controlled for, given the large fraction of leveraged loans in the dataset. The LL dummy is significant at the 1% level and has a negative sign. This negative effect on launch spreads could be due to the higher degree of tranching found for leveraged loan transactions. As this effect should be captured in the number of rating classes, the negative coefficient is surprising, even more so as the LL dummy is also supposed to proxy for information asymmetries. However, due to missing values on the weighted average life (WAL) of the securities, the WAL was not controlled for, even though the WAL should be of importance when analyzing launch spreads. The analysis was equally performed when using the subsample where the WAL is available (not reported), where the sample size reduces to 610 tranches. The WAL is significant for some specifications with a negative coefficient, and removes explanatory power from the LL dummy in models V-VII. The remaining results are almost unchanged.

Again, the share of deal CN variable is added to the set of explanatory variables in model VI and is significant at 1%, while coefficients on all other variables and the R^2 are not largely affected.

In model VII, the rating dummies are dropped and instead the refined rating index is used, capturing more information than the full letter grade rating dummies but on a linear scale. This inclusion of rating refinements removes the size of the coefficient on the credit enhancement and its significance, while there are no substantial changes on the other coefficients.

Summarizing the findings up to this point, four observations can be made. First, rating without refinements explains almost all variation in launch spreads. Second, the level and slope of the yield curve further help to explain launch spreads. However, the effects of the interest rate environment are not fully in line with existing literature and merit further investigation. Third, the equity transfer proxy has the expected sign, and is statistically significant in three out of four specifications. However, the maximum increase in adjusted R^2 by adding

Table 3.10: Launch spreads and risk transfer (ii) – The dependent variable in all regressions is the natural logarithm of each tranche's launch spread, grouped by rating category according to the column headings. OLS is estimated. Heteroscedasticity-robust standard errors are reported in parentheses, with the clustering of tranches within deals being taken into account. All regressions include a constant, which is not reported. Significance of coefficients is indicated as follows: bold coefficients are significant at 0.1%, bold and italic coefficients are significant at 1%, and coefficients with one asterisk are significant at 5%.

	AAA	AA	A	BBB	BB
Share of deal CN	-0.736*	***-1.235***	***-1.472***	-1.175*	***-0.661***
	(0.301)	(0.452)	(0.523)	(0.477)	(0.232)
Yield level	**0.215**	**0.300**	**0.275**	***0.147***	0.033
	(0.041)	(0.053)	(0.060)	(0.049)	(0.031)
Yield slope	**0.348**	**0.402**	**0.467**	**0.294**	**0.406**
	(0.035)	(0.057)	(0.046)	(0.044)	(0.028)
Ln deal volume	0.071	-0.060	**-0.246**	-0.096	-0.063
	(0.048)	(0.083)	(0.066)	(0.053)	(0.053)
Ln tranche volume	**-0.113**	-0.017	0.023	-0.016	-0.057*
	(0.012)	(0.039)	(0.042)	(0.022)	(0.027)
Share of deal FLP	0.957	1.542	1.327	2.290	0.254
	(0.556)	(1.556)	(1.094)	(1.164)	(1.383)
Credit enhancement	**-0.380**	0.195	-0.980	-1.648	-0.646
	(0.093)	(0.222)	(0.591)	(0.941)	(1.133)
Nb rating classes ex CN	0.014	-0.026	0.038	0.011	0.000
	(0.026)	(0.037)	(0.040)	(0.044)	(0.024)
LL dummy	**-0.147**	***-0.304***	-0.175*	-0.075	-0.087
	(0.042)	(0.095)	(0.072)	(0.058)	(0.046)
Sample size	234	128	120	127	104
Adjusted R^2	0.662	0.711	0.690	0.523	0.801
Prob > F	0.000	0.000	0.000	0.000	0.000
Clusters	123	119	116	120	102

the equity transfer proxy is only in the dimension of three-tenth of a percent. And fourth, results on the control variables are in line with expectations.

To better disentangle the effect of observed equity transfer via combination notes on launch spreads, data is rearranged by the rating categories AAA to BB (only six tranches are rated single B), and the regressions are run again within each rating group. Results are reported in table 3.10. All explanatory variables are considered again, though the previously dominating rating information is eliminated by this grouping of data.

Several general observations are of interest. First, the coefficient on the tranche volume is only strongly present for AAA-rated securities. This indicates that on a tranche level post-issue liquidity matters for senior securities only, while markets for lower-rated securities seem to be segmented and the placement of large tranches not beneficial from an issuer perspective. Second, the deal volume has a negative impact on launch spreads of lower-rated tranches, significant for A-rated securities, which is some evidence, that the marketability for not AAA-rated tranches is increasing with the overall deal volume. Third, the credit enhancement is equally only an important determinant of launch spreads for AAA-rated securities, which is a puzzling result, as the credit enhancement should capture additional information versus the credit rating. Inspecting the data reveals that variation within the credit enhancement is only substantial for AAA-rated securities, and credit enhancement levels become more and more similar when moving down the rating grades. Thus, while the level of subordination for senior securities is determined not exclusively by their rating, rating alone seems to capture subordination for lower-rated tranches. Finally, the negative impact of the LL dummy on launch spreads is confirmed for AAA, AA, and A-rated securities. Equally confirmed is the lack of impact of the relative size of the FLP and of the number of rating classes among the plain vanilla tranches on launch spreads.

When looking at the equity transfer proxy, results previously obtained in table 3.9 are confirmed. Coefficients are all negative and significant at 1% and 5%. Adding the WAL to the explanatory variables removes statistical significance from the coefficient on the share of deal CN for AAA-rated securities, and increases the significance of the coefficient for BBB-rated securities to the 1% level (not reported). The interpretation is as follows: the further subordinated a security, the higher the risk of being hit by defaults in the underlying asset pool. The positive quality signal hence gains importance for lower-rated securities, while the effect on senior securities is limited. Economically, an increase of the relative aggregate CN volume by 0.01 implies a decrease of launch spreads in the range of 0.66-1.47%, as indicated by the coefficients in table 3.10 and in line with the results from table 3.9. However, the size of the coefficients is not steadily increasing with decreasing rating. Contrary to the analysis above, adding the share of deal CN variable to the analysis now increases adjusted R^2

noticeably. All regression were equally run without the equity transfer proxies (not reported). Adding the share of deal CN to the analysis increases adjusted R^2 going from AAA to BB by 0.9%, 1.6%, 2.4%, 3.1%, and 0.9%.

Overall, the results indicate that the degree of equity transfer via the issuance of combination notes is observed by market participants and has a positive impact on pricing from the issuer's perspective as launch spreads decrease with rising equity transfer. However, credit ratings explain the large majority of variation in launch spreads, and the observed equity transfer only has a minor impact.

3.5 Conclusion

This is the first empirical article to focus on combination notes issued in securitization transactions. Several results are derived. Considering the descriptive statistics, the amount of overall equity transfer was estimated based on a subsample of the data where the exact combination note compositions are available: on average, about three combination notes are issued per deal, each containing a fraction of 8% deal equity. Together, this implies an equity transfer of € 1.24 billion of overall € 4.9 billion equity via combination notes for the 126 deals considered here. Also for the subsample, the rating of the combination notes is reconsidered: ratings assigned by the rating agencies are better than the value weighted averages of the single components' ratings. However, some of the assigned ratings are principal only ratings, and some ratings are assigned to a so-called rated balance only.

Tranching of combination notes is entirely driven by segmented demand for these securities. When focusing on the tranching decision within the combination notes of a deal, the aggregate volume of the combination notes in that deal is the predominant explanatory variable. When analyzing the tranching decision of combination notes at the deal level, no evidence can be found that tranching of combination notes reduces information asymmetries. Results on the benchmark case, the tranching decision among the plain vanilla tranches, are overall in line with existing literature, though weak in the statistical evidence due to the comparably small sample size. Moreover, there is support that the market for combination notes of a single deal and therefore also equity of a single deal is limited in size, indicated by a negative relation of the overall deal volume and the relative size of combination notes per deal.

Further, equity transfer can be identified as a driver for the issuance of combination notes, as the relative size of the combination notes in a deal increases the lower the quality of the deal. Moreover, equity transfer via combination notes is observed and accounted for by market participants: an impact of equity transfer proxied by combination note properties on launch spreads of plain vanilla tranches was detected. However, the predominant pricing factor for the securities considered here is the credit rating without refinements. The equity transfer information can explain variations in launch spreads when securities are grouped according to their rating, such that pricing factors beyond the credit rating are captured. This refined analysis reveals that observed equity transfer reduces launch spreads especially for securities not rated AAA, while the post-issue liquidity effect associated with a larger tranche size and the credit enhancement only have an impact on the launch spreads of AAA-rated securities. Further, there is some but weak support that the overall deal volume reduces launch spreads for mezzanine securities.

Besides the results described above, several aspects still deserve closer examination. On a descriptive level, a link between issuer sophistication and the issuance of combination notes was established. The analysis of this relation could be extended and generalized by integrating proxies for issuer reputation in the analysis of launch spreads. Also, results on the interest rate environment and its impact on launch spreads are mixed when compared to the literature on changes in bond spreads. Differences are possibly due to the specific characteristics of the underlying assets analyzed here, and merit closer examination. More generally, a comprehensive dataset on the issuance or retention of equity pieces in securitization transactions would allow several interesting research projects. However, the equity piece distribution is unknown even to regulators, and market participants are so far reluctant to release this confidential information.

Appendix for chapter 3

Table 3.11: Rating indices and rating agencies' letter grades

Refined rating index	Rating index	S&P / Fitch	Moody's	Rating factor 10-year maturity
22	10	AAA	Aaa	1
21	9	AA+	Aa1	10
20	9	AA	Aa2	20
19	9	AA-	Aa3	40
18	8	A+	A1	70
17	8	A	A2	120
16	8	A-	A3	180
15	7	BBB+	Baa1	260
14	7	BBB	Baa2	360
13	7	BBB-	Baa3	610
12	6	BB+	Ba1	940
11	6	BB	Ba2	1350
10	6	BB-	Ba3	1766
9	5	B+	B1	2220
8	5	B	B2	2720
7	5	B-	B3	3490
6	4	CCC+	Caa1	4770
5	4	CCC	Caa2	6500
4	4	CCC-	Caa3	8070
3	3	CC	Ca	
2	2	C	C	
1	1	D	default	

Bibliography for chapter 3

Amato, Jeffery / Remolona, Eli (2005): The pricing of unexpected credit losses, Working Paper No. 190, Bank for International Settlements, Basel.

Basel Committee on Banking Supervision (2004): International convergence of capital measurement and capital standards – A revised framework, Basel.

Bluhm, Christian / Overbeck, Ludger / Wagner, Christoph (2003): An introduction to credit risk modeling, London.

Boot, Arnoud / Thakor, Anjan (1993): Security design, in: *Journal of Finance*, Vol. 48, pp. 1349–1378.

Boudoukh, Jacob / Whitelaw, Robert / Richardson, Matthew / Stanton, Richard (1997): Pricing mortgage-backed securities in a multifactor interest rate environment: A multivariate density estimation approach, in: *Review of Financial Studies*, Vol. 10, pp. 405–446.

Brennan, Michael / Hein, Julia / Poon, Ser-Huang (2008): Tranching and pooling, Working Paper, UCLA.

Campbell, John / Taksler, Glen (2003): Equity volatility and corporate bond yields, in: *Journal of Finance*, Vol. 58, pp. 2321–2349.

Collin-Dufresne, Pierre / Goldstein, Robert / Martin, Spencer (2001): The determinants of credit spread changes, in: *Journal of Finance*, Vol. 56, pp. 2177–2207.

DeMarzo, Peter (2005): The pooling and tranching of securities: A model of informed intermediation, in: *Review of Financial Studies*, Vol. 18, pp. 1–35.

Driessen, Joost (2005): Is default event risk priced in corporate bonds?, in: *Review of Financial Studies*, Vol. 18, pp. 165–195.

Duffee, Gregory (1998): The relation between treasury yields and corporate bond yield spreads, in: *Journal of Finance*, Vol. 53, pp. 2225–2241.

Duffie, Darell / Gârleanu, Nicolae (2001): Risk and valuation of collateralized debt obligations, in: *Financial Analysts Journal*, Vol. January/February, pp. 41–59.

Elton, Edwin / Gruber, Martin / Agrawal, Deepak / Mann, Christopher (2001): Explaining the rate spread on corporate bonds, in: *Journal of Finance*, Vol. 56, pp. 247–277.

Firla-Cuchra, Maciej (2005): Explaining launch spreads on structured bonds, Working Paper, University of Oxford.

Firla-Cuchra, Maciej / Jenkinson, Tim (2005): Security design in the real world: Why are securitization issues tranched?, Working Paper, University of Oxford.

Fitch Ratings (2005): Hedge funds: An emerging force in the global credit markets, New York.

Fitch Ratings (2007): Equity and combination notes in cash flow CDOs, New York.

Fitch Ratings (2008): Exposure draft: Retaining equity piece risk – Enhancing transparency, New York.

Franke, Günter / Herrmann, Markus / Weber, Thomas (2007): Information asymmetries and securitization design, Working Paper, University of Konstanz.

Franke, Günter / Weber, Thomas (2007): Wie werden Collateralized Debt Obligation-Transaktionen gestaltet?, in: *Schmalenbachs Zeitschrift für betriebswirtschaftliche Forschung*, Vol. 57/7 (Sonderheft), pp. 95–123.

Gaur, Vishal / Seshadri, Sridhar / Subrahmanyam, Marti (2003): Market incompleteness and super value additivity: Implications for securitization, Working Paper, Stern School of Business, New York.

Gorton, Gary / Pennacchi, George (1995): Banks and loan sales: Marketing nonmarketable assets, in: *Journal of Monetary Economics*, Vol. 35, pp. 389–411.

Gorton, Gary / Souleles, Nicholas (2005): Special purpose vehicles and securitization, Working Paper, Wharton School, Pennsylvania.

Hein, Julia (2006): Optimization of credit enhancements in collateralized loan obligations: The role of loss allocation and reserve account, Working Paper, University of Konstanz.

International Monetary Fund (2006): Global financial stability report. Market developments and issues, Washington D.C., April 2006.

Longstaff, Francis / Schwartz, Eduardo (1995): A simple approach to valuing risky fixed and floating rate debt, in: *Journal of Finance*, Vol. 50, pp. 789–819.

Longstaff, Francis / Rajan, Arvind (2008): An empirical analysis of the pricing of collateralized debt obligations, in: *Journal of Finance*, Vol. 63, pp. 529–563.

Merchant, Shanker (2004): The CDO equity: An emerging class of alternative investments, in: *Journal of Alternative Investments*, Vol. 7, Winter 2004, pp. 47–58.

Moody's Investors Service (2003): Moody's approach to rating synthetic CDOs, New York.

Moody's Investors Service (2004): Using the structured note methodology to rate CDO combo-notes, New York.

Papke, Leslie / Wooldridge, Jeffrey (1996): Econometric methods for fractional response variables with an application to 401(K) plan participation rates, in: *Journal of Applied Econometrics*, Vol. 11, pp. 619–632.

Perraudin, William / Taylor, Alex (2003): Liquidity and bond market spreads, Working Paper, Bank of England.

Plantin, Guillaume (2004): Tranching, Working Paper, Tepper School of Business, Pennsylvania.

Riddiough, Timothy (1997): Optimal design and governance of asset-backed securities, in: *Journal of Financial Intermediation*, Vol. 6, pp. 121–153.

Scheicher, Martin (2008): How has CDO market pricing changed during the turmoil? Evidence from CDS index tranches, ECB Working Paper No. 910, Frankfurt.

Standard & Poor's (2002): Global cash flow and synthetic CDO criteria, New York.

Standard & Poor's (2004): CDO spotlight: Issues in rating combination notes in cash flow CDOs, New York.

Tavakoli, Janet (2003): Collateralized debt obligations & structured finance, New Jersey.

4 Asset pool quality and tranching of CDOs

4.1 Introduction

The securitization of assets has become a standard technique in global financial markets in the last decade. Several assets are pooled to build the collateral for new securities (asset backed securities) which are commonly tranched according to a subordination principle: losses that arise in the collateral pool are assigned to different tranches in a waterfall structure. The most subordinated tranche captures all losses up to its notional amount, further losses are allocated to the next senior tranche, and so on. This mechanism for prioritization of payments results in different ratings for the tranches in securitization transactions. However, the number of differently rated tranches varies significantly across securitization transactions. The purpose of this analysis is to explore the mechanisms that determine the number of differently rated tranches in securitization transactions. The article argues in favor of a simple transaction cost-based determination of the optimal number of differently rated tranches. Given that the spread to be paid on tranches rises with declining rating, issuers should create as many differently rated tranches as possible to minimize overall spread payments. The only constraint to this tranching strategy is that, in case tranches become too small, they are no longer marketable. Since attachment and detachment points for tranche sizes result from the shape of the underlying loss distribution, the quality of the underlying asset pool is the major determinant for the number of differently rated tranches in securitization transactions. Especially for steep ranges of the loss distribution, tranche sizes can become comparably small. Therefore, the number of differently rated tranches is expected to rise with decreasing quality of the underlying asset pool and hence a flatter shape and larger tails of the loss distribution. This transaction cost-based hypothesis on the tranching decision will be elaborated in greater depth in the subsequent sections, with the remainder of this chapter being organized as follows.

Section 4.2 reviews the existing theoretical and empirical literature on the subject. Section 4.3 formulates more generally the expected relationship between the quality of the underlying asset pool and the number of differently rated tranches that are created in securitization transactions. Section 4.4 analyzes the above postulated relationship empirically. The data in general and various available measures of asset pool quality are discussed first to allow an empirical analysis. Based on the transaction cost-based hypothesis of tranching, a simulation is run in section 4.4.3, which predicts the number of differently rated tranches for 191 European collateralized debt obligations (CDOs), a subset of the data. Both simulation results and different asset pool quality measures are used in the empirical analysis in sections 4.4.4 and 4.4.5, with support for the supposed relation of asset pool quality and tranching being strong. Section 4.5 discusses the robustness of the results, section 4.6 summarizes major findings, and section 4.7 concludes the chapter.

4.2 Literature review

4.2.1 Theoretical aspects of tranching

Several articles address the prevalent structural elements of securitization—pooling and tranching—from a theoretical perspective.

Early evidence is provided by Gorton / Pennacchi (1995), who analyze the moral hazard conflict that arises in loan sale transactions: given that a bank sells a loan it originally originated, incentives for adequate monitoring of the debtor decrease as losses no longer accrue to the bank but to the buyer of the loan. In case the bank monitoring level is unobservable, the loan buyer is subject to moral hazard.[1] These distorting incentives can be mitigated by an implicit partial guarantee to buy back the loan in case of default and by the retention of a share of the loan, with the necessary retained fraction being smaller the better

[1] Note that the monitoring effort can be interpreted as either the bank's credit evaluation service prior to loan origination or as monitoring effort in an existing credit relationship; see Gorton / Pennacchi (1995), p. 397.

the quality of the loan to be sold. Transferring these results to securitization transactions, the retained fraction resembles the (commonly retained) first loss piece (FLP); the fraction sold can be thought of as a senior security in terms of securitization. Mitigating the moral hazard conflict hence basically requires a two-security structure, but cannot explain a variety of differently rated tranches.

Boot and Thakor (1993) analyze security design from an issuer perspective. They derive the optimal security design that an issuer implements given that he faces different types of investors. Investors are pure liquidity traders, informed traders, and traders that clear the market by setting the equilibrium price such that they earn zero profits. Boot and Thakor show that it is optimal for a high quality firm to split the financial claims they issue against their cash flows rather than selling a composite security. By issuing an information sensitive security, it is more beneficial for informed traders to invest in information acquisition, thereby better leveraging their own skills. As this enhanced information production drives the price of the information sensitive security closer to its true value, this security design results in a higher overall payoff to the issuer. Conversely, the non-information sensitive security is riskless, and hence information production on that senior security not worth while to investors. Low quality firms are forced to imitate the security design chosen by high quality firms, as their true type would be revealed otherwise. Further, Boot and Thakor argue that even though the optimal number of tranches can exceed two in case of random firm value realizations and in case of more than two types of issuers, it is finite. This is due to the fact that demand rationing may become necessary to preclude type verification by order sizes, which can result in reduced informed demand.[2] For more than two different types of issuers, Boot and Thakor expect a rising number of securities with rising asset quality. However, lower quality firms would imitate high quality firms in a pooling equilibrium of the kind presented for the two issuer case by Boot and Thakor, which raises difficulties in an empirical validation.

Riddiough's (1997) model of asset securitization does not provide further insights in the context of this study. The number of tranches to be created (two

[2] See Boot / Thakor (1993), p. 1365.

or three) depends entirely on the severity of the internal capital constraint that drives the entire transaction. Further, the crucial point in the three tranche solution is the smaller size of the FLP but not the existence of two senior securities.

Plantin (2004) suggests a model similar to Boot and Thakor (1993). He focuses on an investment bank that arranges a private placement. The bank faces different investors: investors with good screening skills but bad redistribution skills, and investors with bad screening skills but good redistribution skills (investors need to redistribute the securities they acquire). Plantin analyzes different settings. In case information asymmetry on the underlying assets pool is low, a junior security must be created to attract the investors with good screening skills to participate in the transactions. In case information asymmetry is high, a senior security must be created to protect the investors with bad screening skills from competing with those having good screening skills and hence to avoid the Winner's Curse. Plantin extends the model to an investment bank facing more than two different investors. The optimal number of tranches rises with the number of different investors. Investor sophistication decreases with increasing seniority of the securities they bid for.

DeMarzo (2005) likewise describes an adverse selection setting in the context of asset securitization, where the retention of the FLP resolves the agency conflict in a signaling game. DeMarzo focuses on two opposing effects from pooling: an information destruction effect and a diversification effect. Pooling and tranching is beneficial if benefits due to diversification overcompensate the information destruction effect, with this result holding for a multiple-tranche setting as well.

Gaur / Seshadri / Subrahmanyam (2003) focus on market incompleteness. They show that, in a market where some but not all assets can be priced uniquely, singling out new cash flow profiles increases market spanning and is rewarded by a premium. They allow for multiple tranches when applying their model to securitization, with the optimal transaction structure arising from an optimization algorithm.

Overall, there is strong support for the creation of at least two tranches in securitization transactions, be it due to information asymmetries or in order to incentivize sophisticated market participants to participate in the market and hence to produce valuable screening effort. The creation of multiple securities does not compete with the two-security structure, and is addressed by most of the articles mentioned above, even though it is not their main focus. The hypothesis to be derived in this article does not rely on the results above, but on a transaction cost-based approach, and does more strongly focus on the number of differently rated tranches in securitization transactions.

4.2.2 Existing empirical evidence on tranching

Empirical evidence on pooling and tranching is still limited to a small set of papers. Firla-Cuchra / Jenkinson (2005) (henceforth C/J) provide a comprehensive empirical analysis on the tranching decision of ABS. C/J find several determinants for the tranching decisions. They show that tranching increased over time with the time dimension being a proxy for increasing investor sophistication. Further, C/J distinguish differently rated tranches (rating classes) and additional tranches that do not distinguish themselves by rating (market classes). The number of rating classes is the number of different ratings (taking into account refinements) in a structure, while the number of market classes is the overall number of tranches minus the number of rating classes. Non-rated tranches are considered to be market classes.[3] 'Differently rated tranches' and 'rating classes' are hence synonyms. The number of rating classes is shown to be higher with higher information asymmetries, while segmented primary markets and illiquid secondary markets have a stronger impact on the number of market classes. Concerning the quality of the underlying asset pool, the impact on the number of rating classes is ambiguous, while the number of market classes decreases with rising quality of the underlying asset pool. Asset pool quality is measured as value weighted average of the tranches' ratings for each deal.

[3] To take an example, a transaction with two AAA tranches, one AA+ tranche, two AA tranches, one BBB tranche, and one non-rated FLP has four rating classes and three market classes.

Franke / Weber (2007) derive and analyze various hypotheses on the relation of the quality of the underlying asset pool and several structuring decisions. Among other results they find that asset pools are better diversified for CLO transactions than for CBO transactions, and also better diversified for synthetic than for true sale transactions. Moreover they find that the relative size of the FLP is increasing in the average default probability and increasing with decreasing diversification of the underlying asset pool.[4] Further, and most interestingly for this study, they find that the number of differently rated tranches increases with an increasing average default probability, but also with an increasing diversity score (a measure of asset pool diversification provided by Moody's), hence with a higher degree of diversification. Franke / Herrmann / Weber (2007) extend the analysis provided by Franke and Weber. They additionally find that the relative size of the senior security in synthetic transactions decreases with a rising average default probability, and increases with rising diversification.

In chapter 3 of this thesis, I analyze combination notes, a specific type of note issued in some securitization transactions, which comprise parts of several tranches from the same transaction. This research provides the first documented empirical evidence that CDO equity is (partly) sold to market participants. Tranching of combination notes is purely driven by segmented markets, combination notes apparently are only marketable in certain tranche sizes.

4.3 Derivation of a transaction cost-based hypothesis of the number of differently rated tranches

The idea to be derived here is akin to the idea formulated in C/J, however with a different implication for the relation of asset pool quality and tranching.[5] C/J argue that the originator of a securitization transaction should create the maximum number of tranches as he likely faces segmented demand, and can therefore enhance the investor base and avoid negative effects of tranche sizes on their price on the primary market. However, extensive tranching could be prohibited by

4 This relation only holds for a regression that takes into account the diversity score and its reciprocal value.

5 See Firla-Cuchra / Jenkinson (2005), pp. 17-18 for the following paragraph.

various costs that are associated with tranching, such as legal, regulatory, servicing, and rating agencies costs, but also liquidity costs on secondary markets in case tranches become too small. C/J use the deal amount to test their hypothesis: larger deals should be tranched more to exploit different market segments, whereas smaller deals should be tranched less in order to preserve post-issue liquidity. C/J find strong support for their hypothesis in their data. The number of market as well as rating classes rises with rising deal volume, with the impact being stronger on the number of market classes.

I argue that the number of differently rated tranches (rating classes in C/J) is mostly driven by the financial engineering process inherent in the creation of securitization transactions. Principally, an originator should create the maximum possible number of differently rated tranches to reduce the costs of the transaction in terms of spread payments. The level of spreads to pay is determined on the one hand by actual market conditions and on the other hand by the probabilities of default (and/or the expected losses) of the relevant tranches which translate into different ratings, with a lower probability of default and hence a better rating naturally requiring lower spread payments.[6] The lowest overall spread payments on a given deal can hence be achieved by creating as many differently rated tranches as possible. However, as mentioned in C/J, tranching is costly. I argue that all operational costs mentioned above occur mostly on the deal level and are not strongly affected by the creation of an additional tranche. However, there is a minimum size that tranches must have in order to be marketable at all. The minimum size exists due to different reasons. From an investor's point of view research is costly and only worth while in case the tranche size exceeds a certain volume. From an originator's point of view the same argument holds for marketing efforts. Further, the preservation of a tranche's post-issue liquidity by not creating too small tranches, as proposed in C/J, reinforces the existence of a minimum necessary tranche size. In case the tranche size is the only limiting factor for the placement of a tranche, the number of differently rated tranches will strongly depend on the shape of the

[6] Firla-Cuchra (2005) finds that rating alone explains 71.9% and 78.1% of the variation in launch spreads for floating rate and fixed rate notes. The Bank of England also reports a strong reliance on ratings, see Bank of England (2007), pp. 53-54.

loss distribution of the underlying asset pool, as the shape of the loss distribution determines the attachment and detachment points for the tranches to be engineered. While senior tranches will, for realistic parameter constellations, not become too small to be marketable, mezzanine tranches can become small in case the underlying assets are well diversified so that the loss distribution is concentrated around the expected loss.

The shape of the loss distribution is determined by the probability of default of the underlying assets and the correlation structure in the asset pool. An increase in the probability of default of the underlying asset pool shifts the expected loss to a higher loss rate (to the right) and results in lower values for the distribution function of losses for all loss rates. This shift in the distribution function thus implies a larger first loss piece and a smaller senior security. An increase in the correlation among the underlying assets shifts probability mass into the tails of the loss distribution, resulting in a distribution function that slopes out more steeply for low loss rates, but thereafter flattens out more strongly for high loss rates. The effect of such a shift in the distribution function on the size of the tranches depends on the point of intersection for the distribution functions for different correlation parameters, but is likely to lead to a smaller senior security and larger mezzanine tranches. These relations are illustrated more generally in the following drawing on the assumption of a large homogeneous portfolio (LHP). Throughout the remainder of the analysis, tranching is based on the probability of default of tranches and not on expected losses; I thus follow the rating practice of Standard & Poor's.[7] The large homogeneous portfolio consists of $m \to \infty$ loans, which all have the same (unconditional) probability of default p and a uniform asset correlation of ϱ in a one-factor model. Assuming further an LGD of 100%, the distribution function for the portfolio loss rate L is, for $0 \leq x \leq 1$, given by[8]

[7] See Standard & Poor's (2007). See also Brennan / Hein / Poon (2008) for an analysis of arbitrage-driven CDOs for ratings that are based on probabilities of default as well as ratings that are based on expected losses.

[8] See Bluhm / Overbeck / Wagner (2003), pp. 83-99 for a detailed derivation of the distribution properties for the large homogeneous portfolio and for a more rigorous discussion of the underlying assumptions.

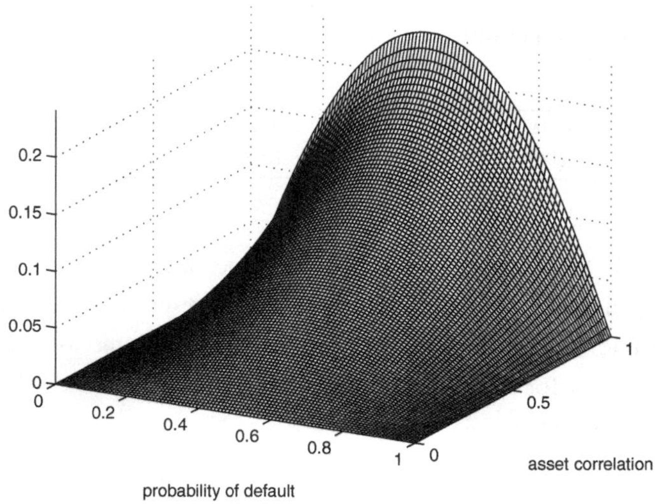

Figure 4.1: Variance of loss distribution LHP as function of p and ϱ

$$F_{p,\varrho}(x) = P[L \leq x] = \Phi\left[\frac{\Phi^{-1}(x)\sqrt{1-\varrho} - \Phi^{-1}(p)}{\sqrt{\varrho}}\right] , \tag{4.1}$$

where Φ denotes the distribution function of a standard normal variable. The mean and variance for the portfolio loss rate are given by

$$E[L] = p \quad \text{and} \quad V[L] = \Phi_2[\Phi^{-1}(p), \Phi^{-1}(p); \varrho] - p^2 ,$$

where $\Phi_2[\cdot, \cdot; \varrho]$ denotes the bivariate standard normal distribution function with correlation ϱ. The behavior of the variance of the loss rate $V[L]$ is plotted in figure 4.1. The variance of the loss rate (and hence the unexpected loss) rises with rising correlation in the underlying asset pool. The behavior of the variance towards the unconditional probability of default is symmetric around $p = 0.5$: below $p = 0.5$ the variance rises in p, above $p = 0.5$ the variance decreases in p.

As can be seen from equation (4.1), an increase in p reduces the value of $F_{p,\varrho}$ for a given value of ϱ, and therefore implies a first order stochastic dom-

Table 4.1: Moody's cumulative default rate (one year time horizon) by rating 1920-2004 in %

Aaa	Aa	A	Baa	Ba	B	Caa-C
0.0001	0.06	0.08	0.31	1.39	4.56	15.07

inance shift in the loss rate distribution.[9] An increase in the asset correlation from ϱ to $\tilde{\varrho}$, holding p constant, leads to a mean-preserving spread of the loss rate distribution, hence the loss rates intersect once at some loss rate x^*, and $F_{p,\tilde{\varrho}}(x) > F_{p,\varrho}(x)$ for $x < x^*$ and $F_{p,\tilde{\varrho}}(x) < F_{p,\varrho}(x)$ for $x > x^*$. The point of intersection is given by

$$x^* = \Phi\left[\frac{\Phi^{-1}(p)(\sqrt{\varrho}-\sqrt{\tilde{\varrho}})}{\sqrt{1-\tilde{\varrho}}\sqrt{\varrho}-\sqrt{1-\varrho}\sqrt{\tilde{\varrho}}}\right] . \tag{4.2}$$

The proof concerning the mean-preserving spread can be found in appendix A. The impact of both the first order stochastic dominance shift and the mean-preserving spread on the tranching of the deal will depend on the parameter values for the probability of default p and the asset correlation ϱ. For a sub-sample of 191 of the deals to be analyzed subsequently, proxies for p and ϱ are available. For these transactions, I consider both a one-standard deviation shift in p and in ϱ within the LHP framework in the following, assuming a one year maturity for the securities as the proxies for p and ϱ are annualized values, and furthermore an LGD of 100%. The attachment points for the tranches are based on the default rates presented in table 4.1.

The shift in p, holding ϱ fixed, results in an increase in the size of the FLP and a decrease in the size of the senior security (AAA). For all 191 deals, the distance between the detachment point of the FLP and the attachment point of the senior security increases, hence, the absolute impact of the increase of p by one standard deviation on the senior security is larger than the impact on the junior security. The mean-preserving spread induced by a one-standard deviation

[9] See Franke / Herrmann / Weber (2007), p. 12 and pp. 53-54 for the same arguments concerning first and second order stochastic dominance shifts for changes in p and ϱ relying on a lognormal distribution.

increase in ϱ results in 42 points of intersection x^* that are located inside the interval bounded by the detachment point of the FLP and the attachment point of the senior security, and 149 points of intersection that are located within the FLP. The effect of an increase in the asset correlation on the FLP is hence ambiguous. No single point of intersection is located within the AAA security, hence the size of the AAA security decreases due to the increase in the asset correlation. Furthermore, the overall effect of the increase in ϱ on the distance between the detachment point of the FLP and the attachment point of the senior security is positive for all 191 deals within the LHP framework. Comparing the one-standard deviation increases in p and ϱ, the absolute impact of p on the size of the FLP is about four times stronger than the impact of ϱ.[10] Concerning the absolute impact on the size of the senior security, the impact of the increase in ϱ is 2.5 times higher than the impact of p. Overall, the increase in the distance between the detachment point of the FLP and the attachment point of the senior security is about three times larger for the increase in ϱ.

Given these properties of the loss distribution and given the conjecture that transactions are tranched to minimize transaction costs, I expect the following hypotheses to hold:

> *H1*: The number of differently rated tranches rises with increasing correlation and increasing probability of default of the underlying asset pool, hence with an overall decreasing quality of the underlying asset pool. The impact of an increase in the asset correlation is stronger than the impact of an increase in the probability of default.

> *H2*: The size of the FLP increases with an increasing probability of default in the underlying asset pool.

> *H3*: The size of the senior security decreases for both an increase in the probability of default and an increase in the asset correlation in the underlying asset pool.

[10] I compare the averages of the absolute effects.

H1 is the major hypothesis of this analysis and is opposed to Firla-Cuchra / Jenkinson (2005), who expect a rising number of differently rated tranches given an increase in the quality of the underlying asset pool. H2 and H3 are formulated to enhance the understanding of the financial engineering inherent in asset securitization and hence to support H1.

To illustrate the underlying mechanics, the density and distribution function is drawn for three large homogeneous sample portfolios. It is assumed that the single securities are zero bonds with a one year maturity. One distribution function is drawn for a uniform probability of default of 0.025 and an asset correlation of 0.13, which roughly corresponds to the sample means. For the two other distribution functions, the probability of default or the asset correlation are increased by approximately one standard deviation. Again, an LGD of 100% is assumed, I furthermore abstract from any cash flow modeling, and the loss distributions are tranched based on the probability of default. Hence, the portfolio loss rate that is exceeded only with a probability linked to a certain rating determines the attachment point of a tranche. The default probabilities used are taken from Moody's (2005) and are historical default rates of corporate bonds from the time period 1920-2004. They are displayed in table 4.1.[11] As the one-year default rate for Aaa-rated securities is not verifiable in exhibit 17 in Moody's (2005) I instead use the idealized default probability of 0.0001% found in Moody's (2003). Figure 4.2 illustrates the above discussed behavior of the distribution function for portfolio losses at its lower end for a range of the loss rate from 0 to 0.1. The attachment points for the CCC and B rating are captured by the intersections of the distribution functions with the horizontal lines, with the tranche sizes resulting from the distance between the attachment point and the attachment point of the next senior tranche (i.e. the detachment point). The junior security is, in the approach taken here, the distance from zero to the loss rate that is hit at the CCC attachment point. For the shift in ϱ it can be seen that the point of intersection x^* lies just within the FLP. For both the increase in p and in ϱ, the next senior security increases in its size. The behavior of the

[11] Rating letters subsequently used in the text primarily adhere to the notation of Standard & Poor's and Fitch but could equally be those from Moody's.

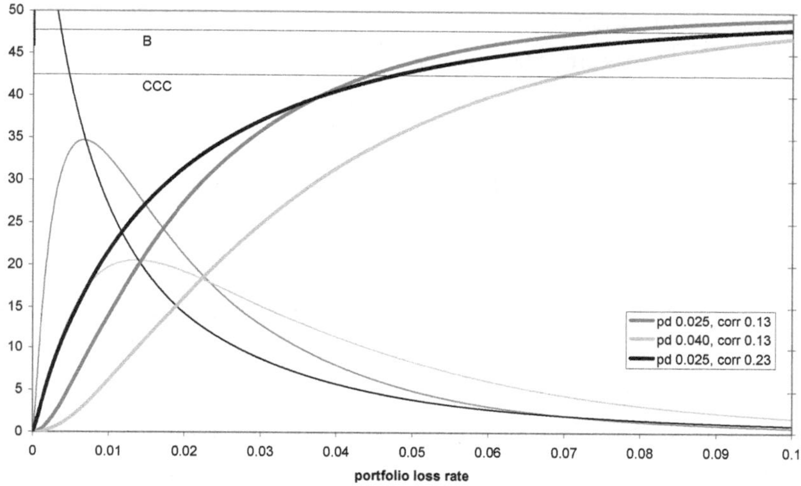

Figure 4.2: LHP density and distribution functions for different values of p and ϱ

remaining tranches is not illustrated in this cutout of the distribution function, but the size of the senior security decreases for both the shifts in p and ϱ.

Two remarks are necessary. First, cash flow modeling is not taken into account in the derivation of the hypotheses. While the existence of structural elements such as a reserve account and excess spread naturally has an impact on tranching, these structural elements are highly transaction-specific and thus cannot be integrated in a general manor.[12] Further, an empirical verification is not possible as data on such structural elements is not available. Second, I abstract from transaction motives like refinancing needs, risk management objectives, and arbitrage. For risk management and arbitrage-driven transactions full tranching is important. Given that significant risk transfer shall be achieved, mezzanine tranches need to be sold. For arbitrage-driven transactions, selling the entire capital structure is vital for the economics of the deal. Only in case of refinancing needs could one argue that funding needs could be met by only selling a senior security, making the creation of further differently rated tranches obsolete. However, to achieve a fixed amount of funding, a lower quality deal

[12] See Hein (2006) on internal credit enhancements.

will require at least as many tranches as a higher quality deal. Therefore, even though not all tranches are to be sold, the relation of pool quality and the number of differently rated tranches is expected to hold.

4.4 Empirical analysis of asset pool quality and tranching

4.4.1 The dataset

I use a dataset on European CDO transactions compiled from an internal database at HypoVereinsbank/UniCredit Global Research, which is fed by various sources such as Moody's, Standard & Poor's, Fitch, Reuters, and Bloomberg. The dataset contains 1021 CDO transactions, and deceases in size to 805 transactions after all single-tranche deals have been excluded. Single-tranche deals are excluded as they are likely to be tailor-made for a single investor. The 805 transactions contain 5055 tranches, the average deal size is € 869 million, and the data spans a period from October 1997 to July 2008. Further, 220 deals are backed by leveraged loans (LL), 235 by SME loans, and the remaining 350 deals are backed by bonds, CLOs and CDOs. To distinguish these subcategories within the segment of CDOs, a leveraged loan and an SME dummy are created. They take the value of one in case a deal is backed by leveraged loans/SME loans, and zero otherwise. Both the LL dummy as well as the SME dummy can be considered as a proxy for information asymmetries in the sense of Franke / Weber (2007), because information on the underlying assets is not publicly available, while information on bonds but also on CDOs and CLOs is available to some extent. Further, pools of SME loans are more granular. The LL dummy is used to disentangle the SME loans from leveraged loans, as they differ in size and characteristics. Ratings are available on the majority of tranches and have been translated to numerical values according to table 4.9 in appendix B, which facilitates their further use. Two scales have been used, one that only contains full letter grades, the *rating index*, and one that considers rating refinements as well, the *refined rating index*. In case ratings from several rating agencies are available, ratings were averaged, with split ratings nonetheless playing a minor role. Furthermore, the number of differently rated

Table 4.2: Summary statistics on the number of tranches

Variable	Mean	Std. Dev.	Min.	Max.	N
Nb tranches	6.28	2.756	2	20	805
Nb rating classes	3.824	1.42	1	8	799
Nb market classes	2.477	2.175	0	16	799

tranches, the rating classes, and the number of market classes were extracted based on the refined rating index. Summary statistics of these variables are given in table 4.2.[13] The number of differently rated tranches ranges from one to eight and averages at 3.82. The maximum number of market classes is by far larger at 16, with the average being only at 2.48.

As proposed in section 4.3, high asset pool quality implies small tranche sizes for mezzanine tranches and might hence prohibit the creation of tranches. In case one or several mezzanine tranches are not created due to their size, 'jumps' in the rating structure of the deal should result. That is, starting from e.g. an AAA-rated senior tranche, not every subsequent rating grade (AA+, AA, AA–, etc.) will be found in the deal. Theses jumps are tabulated in table 4.3. The jumps are derived as the distance on the refined rating index from one tranche to the next senior in the subordination structure of each deal. No jumps can be calculated for the most senior tranches and tranches that do not carry a rating; the total number of rating-jumps therefore levels at 3516 only. It can be seen that there is a large share of zero-notch jumps, which are additional same-rated tranches. Further, only 5.2% of jumps are of one rating notch. There are a large number of jumps of two and three notches. The distance from AAA to AA is two on the refined index, while the distance between all other full letter grades is three (e.g. from AA to A, A to BBB, etc.). However, 175 out of the 588 two-notch jumps are not AAA to AA jumps, and 227 out of the 939 three-notch jumps are not jumps from one full letter grade to the next. Overall, there are 948 jumps that are greater than one and not associated with a jump from one

[13] The number of rating and market classes could not be extracted in case no rating was available, hence N differs for the number of overall tranches and the number of rating and market classes.

Table 4.3: Frequency of rating-jumps

Jumps	>6	6	5	4	3	2	1	0	total
Freq.	75	70	126	275	939	588	183	1260	3516
Percent	2.13	1.99	3.58	7.82	26.71	16.72	5.20	35.84	100.00

full letter rating grade to the next, which can be seen as an initial support for the above formulated hypothesis on tranching.

Only little data will be used that is not deal-specific in the empirical analysis. The time dimension, associated with increasing investor sophistication, will be controlled for by integrating the year of the issue into the analysis. Further, actual bond market conditions need to be taken into account, as they might have a substantial impact on the tranching decision: one can suspect less tranches to be created in case spread levels increase, as transactions become more expensive from the issuer perspective. While C/J use the level of government bond yields and a slope proxy for the yield curve, I propose using spread levels directly from the CDO market.[14] This is due to two reasons. First, even though yields of government bonds have an impact on market conditions in the ABS market, using launch spreads of the relevant market segment itself is a more precise measure of market conditions. Second, results concerning the impact of bond market yields on launch spreads of ABS are ambiguous, see for example the opposing results in Firla-Cuchra (2005) and in chapter 3 of this thesis. Therefore, spreads used in this study are taken from the data itself and hence from the CDO market.[15] Overall, there are 3456 launch spreads available in the data. For each full letter grade rating I ran piecewise linear regressions of launch spreads on the time dimension and predict the launch spreads according to the rating categories. The knots for the piecewise linear regression were set at 10%-quantiles of the data. Correlations of the predicted launch spreads are high between the different rating categories, and any of the time series could be

14 Franke / Weber (2007) do not control for the market conditions in their analysis of differently rated tranches.

15 Similarly, I could have used iTraxx or CDX spreads: inspection of the data reveals that the difference between the iTraxx Europe and the predicted spread for AAA-rated tranches is on average at 1.3 basis points, with a standard deviation of 14 basis points. However, iTraxx index spreads are not available for the full time period.

chosen for the empirical analysis. I particularly proxy the actual market conditions by the difference in fitted BBB and AAA launch spreads. This is due to two reasons. First, both the data on AAA and on BBB spreads is sufficient to run the piecewise regressions. Second, especially more subordinated tranches might not be issued in case spreads are comparably high. Therefore I use the spread on BBB-rated tranches, hence those tranches just at investment grade, but control for general market conditions on the CDO market by subtracting the AAA level of spreads.

4.4.2 Available measures of asset pool quality

Different asset pool quality measures have been used in existing empirical research, while additional measures are provided by rating agencies. C/J use a measure based on the tranching of each deal. They calculate a value weighted average of the tranches' ratings for each deal. Ratings without refinements are translated into a numerical value, with AAA corresponding to six, AA to five etc. Non-rated tranches and hence the FLP correspond to zero. C/J fix the numerical value for AAA at six as there are virtually no tranches rated below B in their data. I equally calculate an *average rating* based on the rating index, hence with AAA tranches being assigned a ten, AA tranches a nine, etc., and non-rated tranches and thus the FLP being assigned a four, as, in my data as well, virtually no tranche is rated below B.[16] While the average rating is a reasonable starting point, I argue that a measure based on the tranches' ratings for each deal could be improved by using a non-linear aggregation of the tranches' ratings, as risk also rises in a non-linear fashion with decreasing rating. I propose using rating factors that are assigned to each rating and tabulated by Moody's to calculate a weighted average rating factor (WARF) for each deal.[17] The weighted average rating factor is hence now based on the ratings of each deal's tranches, and not on the underlying assets' individual ratings, as it is in its original use by

[16] In the data, 21 out of 5055 tranches are rated below B.

[17] The rating factors can be derived from idealized default probabilities published by Moody's and depend on the relevant ratings and maturities. The idealized default probabilities can be found in Moody's (2003), while the mapping of ratings and rating factors for a ten year maturity used here can be found in table 4.9 in appendix B.

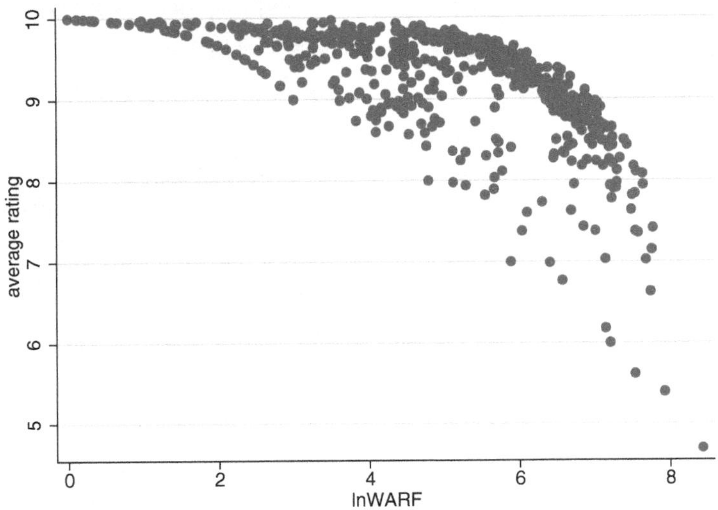

Figure 4.3: Scatterplot of the average rating vs. the lnWARF

Moody's. Non-rated tranches are treated as if rated CCC (corresponding to the value of four on the rating index), and hence assigned a rating factor of 6500. The derived weighted average of rating factors could be translated back into ratings by using table 4.9 in appendix B, but I prefer taking the natural logarithm to derive the variable *lnWARF*, as no information is lost with that approach. Figure 4.3 plots the average rating against the lnWARF and illustrates that the lnWARF provides a considerably more refined ordering of deals.

It is important to keep in mind that both the lnWARF and the average rating are endogenous with respect to tranching. Further, both measures cannot disentangle default probabilities and correlation structures of the underlying asset pool. More refined measures have been used by Franke / Weber (2007), who use two measures provided by Moody's: the diversity score (DS) and a weighted average default probability. The diversity score is derived from the industry concentration of the underlying asset pool and is a measure of pool diversification. It is the crucial input parameter for Moody's binomial expansion technique (BET) but not a formal (statistical) measure of correlation.[18] The weighted average default probability is derived by Franke and Weber from the WARF of the underlying asset pool provided by Moody's by using Moody's idealized default probability tables.

Measures so far not considered in empirical research are those provided by Standard & Poor's. S&P publish a *default measure* (spdef) and a *variability measure* (spvar). These measures are based on the "expected portfolio default rate (EPDR)", and the standard deviation (SD) of the portfolio default rate, both described in Standard & Poor's (2001). The EPDR is the "weighted average portfolio default rate" that "reflects the actual remaining life of the assets"[19]. The standard deviation of the portfolio default rate is defined as

$$SD = \sqrt{\sum_{i=1}^{N}\sum_{j=1}^{N} x_i x_j \sqrt{p_i(1-p_i)}\sqrt{p_j(1-p_j)}\rho_{ij}} = \sqrt{\sum_{i=1}^{N}\sum_{j=1}^{N} x_i x_j \sigma_{ij}} \,, \quad (4.3)$$

where x denotes an asset's share of the portfolio, p is an asset's default rate according to rating and maturity, and ρ_{ij} is the pairwise default correlation of two assets i and j.[20] Given that defaults are Bernoulli distributed, $p(1-p)$ is the variance of the default probability, and the above formula reduces to the common portfolio variance formula, with σ_{ij} being the covariance of two assets i and j. Pairwise default correlation coefficients depend on the instruments' ratings and correlations among industry sectors the instruments belong to and have been estimated based on historical data.[21] The S&P default and variability measure are the annualized versions of the expected portfolio default rate and its standard deviation.[22] The default and the variability measure are available for 191 deals. Summary statistics can be found in table 4.4. They will be used directly as measures of asset pool quality in this study. Additionally,

[18] See Fender / Kiff (2004) for a comparison of the BET to a Monte Carlo approach in rating CDOs.

[19] See Standard & Poor's (2001), p. 2.

[20] See Standard & Poor's (2001), p. 5 for equation (4.3).

[21] See Standard & Poor's (2005), pp. 8-9 and the references therein.

[22] See Standard & Poor's (2006), p. 79 for descriptions.

Table 4.4: Summary statistics on the S&P measures and correlations, $N = 191$

Variable	Mean	Std. Dev.	Min.	Max.
S&P default measure (spdef)	0.0267	0.0154	0.0002	0.0652
S&P variability measure (spvar)	0.0205	0.0084	0.0014	0.0385
Asset correlation (ϱ)	0.1315	0.0979	0.0452	0.5162
Default correlation (ρ)	0.0199	0.0119	0.0032	0.0817

they are used to extract asset correlations for each deal, which will be used as input parameters in the following simulation on the number of differently rated tranches.

The default measure and the variability measure are both on average significantly higher for the subset of leveraged loan transactions than for the remainder of the data, which should be suspected given the nature of leveraged loans, and which confirms the decision to include a leveraged loan dummy in the subsequent empirical analysis.

4.4.3 A simulation of the number of differently rated tranches

To explore the relation of pool quality and tranching a simulation is run that predicts the number of differently rated tranches. Input parameters are probabilities of default for the underlying assets, asset correlation coefficients, probabilities of default that determine the attachment and detachment points for the tranches, and 1%-quantiles of real tranche sizes that determine minimum tranche sizes.

First, a loss distribution is simulated for each deal using a one-factor approach.[23] Each underlying portfolio is assumed to consist of 100 assets with identical exposure at default. Each single asset value A_i is determined by a common factor Z and an idiosyncratic component ε_i

$$A_i = \sqrt{\varrho} Z + \sqrt{1-\varrho}\varepsilon_i \ , \tag{4.4}$$

$$\text{with } cov(\varepsilon_i, \varepsilon_j) = 0 \text{ for } i \neq j \text{ and } cov(Z, \varepsilon_i) = 0, \ \forall i,$$

[23] A one-factor model is equally employed by Krahnen / Wilde (2008), Hamerle / Jobst / Schropp (2008), and Gibson (2004).

and Z and ε_i both being standard normal variables. ϱ is the uniform asset correlation between asset values. In the one-factor approach a default occurs when the asset value falls below a certain threshold d_i,

$$A_i \leq d_i,$$

which is calibrated to the probability of default of the asset by setting $d_i = \Phi^{-1}(p_i)$. In case of default, a random loss given default was implemented using beta-distributed LGDs, where the parameters α and β of the beta distribution were calibrated to an expectation of 0.45 and a standard deviation of 0.3.[24] To obtain the tranching of the loss distribution, quantiles from the simulated loss distribution are derived. Here, two different choices are implemented. The relevant confidence levels are on the one hand derived from table 4.1, which only includes full letter grade ratings, and hence implies a maximum number of seven differently rated tranches. For that choice, the loss distribution is simulated 200,000 times for each portfolio.[25] On the other hand, confidence levels are, again for a one year horizon, derived from Standard & Poor's (2005). The cumulative default probabilities provided in S&P (2005) range from AAA to CCC– (including all refinements) and are those employed in the tool "CDO evaluator". This approach implies a maximum number of 19 differently rated tranches.[26] For that choice, the loss distribution is simulated one million times for each deal. I chose confidence levels that are based on one year default probabilities, as the input parameters are annualized values. By using the above procedure it is assumed that assets are zero bonds, with defaults occurring at the end of their maturity. A more precise estimate of the loss distribution could be derived by modeling coupon paying securities and thus taking into account the timing of defaults. However, no data is available on the frequency and size of coupons for the underlying portfolios. Furthermore, the maturity is likewise

[24] See Löffler / Posch (2007), pp. 139-141 and De Servigny / Renault (2004), pp. 138-141.

[25] Given the low level of default probabilities for the one year horizon, a comparably high number of simulations is necessary to produce reliable simulation results.

[26] Note that it is not obvious which probabilities of default are employed in CDO rating approaches by the different rating agencies. Further, the quantitative meaning of rating letter grades changes across different asset classes. See Nomura (2006) for a market participant's view of this issue.

unavailable for a subset of the data. Therefore, comparing asset values generated by the one-factor model only once to the default threshold based on the one year default rates should be a sufficient modeling approach for the purpose pursued here.

The resulting quantiles determine the attachment and detachment points for the tranches. To take an example: the attachment point for a BBB-rated tranche for the tranching without refinements is given by the 99.69%-quantile, and the detachment point by the 99.92%-quantile of the loss distribution. The tranches obtained by the simulation procedure are expressed as a percentage value of the overall pool volume and multiplied with the real transaction volume of the deal. The size of the resulting tranches is then compared to thresholds for the minimum size of tranches. These thresholds for the minimum tranche sizes are derived from the entire dataset, hence from 5055 tranches. They are the 1%-quantiles of tranche sizes per rating category.[27] In case a tranche is smaller than the threshold for its minimal size, it is expected not to be marketable and thus assumed to not be created. The number of differently rated tranches per deal is the number of tranches that exceed the threshold for their minimal size.

Using this method, the following, which is especially relevant for more junior tranches, is not taken into account. Two or more adjacent tranches could each individually fail to reach the threshold for their minimal size. Combining these adjacent tranches could however result in a tranche that fulfils the minimum threshold for its size for the lowest rating category of the adjacent tranches. Such a tranching decision would imply paying higher spreads than suggested for a certain range of the loss distribution. Whether or not adjacent tranches would be combined will hence depend strongly on the motives for each individual deal, and is therefore not considered in the simulation.

Concerning the input parameters, the probability of default is set at the default measure provided by S&P, thus uniform for all assets in the pool at the average probability of default. As a consequence, the variance for each single default is uniform as well at $spdef(1-spdef)$. The asset correlation ϱ and

[27] The quantiles are derived according to the relevant rating scale, hence once per full letter rating grade and once per refined rating.

hence the factor sensitivity $\sqrt{\varrho}$ is extracted from the variability measure. The variability measure, as described above, contains a measure of pairwise default correlation among assets and can be written as the sum of variances and the sum of covariances

$$spvar^2 = \frac{1}{N}\sum_{i=1}^{N}\frac{\sigma_i^2}{N} + \frac{N-1}{N}\sum_{i=1}^{N}\sum_{\substack{j=1 \\ i\neq j}}^{N}\frac{\sigma_{ij}}{N(N-1)} \ .$$

N defines the number of assets in the portfolio, where it is assumed that all assets are the same size. For the extraction of the asset correlation N is set to 2000, which is close to the median of the number of loans in the underlying portfolios for the data analyzed in this study.[28] Defining the first summation as the average variance $\overline{\sigma}_i^2$ and the second summation as average covariance $\overline{\sigma}_{ij}$, the average covariance is given by

$$\overline{\sigma}_{ij} = \frac{N}{N-1}(spvar^2 - \frac{1}{N}spdef(1-spdef)) \ ,$$

which leads to an average default correlation of

$$\overline{\rho}_{ij} = \frac{\overline{\sigma}_{ij}}{spdef(1-spdef)} \ .$$

The average default correlation in turn can be used to derive the joint default probability $\overline{p}_{ij}$ for any two assets, which is defined by

$$\text{Prob}(A_i \leq d_i, A_j \leq d_j) = \overline{p}_{ij} = \Phi_2(d_i, d_j, \overline{\varrho}_{ij}) \ . \tag{4.5}$$

Relation (4.5) can be used to extract the asset correlation $\overline{\varrho}_{ij}$. This procedure was used to extract uniform asset correlation coefficients for those 191 deals where the S&P measures have been available. Summary statistics are presented in table 4.4.

Overall, the simulation results in two different estimates for the number of differently rated tranches: tranching based on ratings with and without refine-

[28] There are only nine deals where both the S&P measures and the number of loans is available in the dataset. A more precise integration of the number of loans is thus not possible.

ments. The simulated numbers of differently rated tranches will be used as explanatory variables in the regression analysis below.

4.4.4 Empirical findings on the tranching decision

In order to test the relation of asset pool quality and tranching I run several ordered logistic regressions, with the number of differently rated tranches being the dependent variable. As there are only nine deals with more than six differently rated tranches, I reclassify these deals as having six differently rated tranches (which is the 98%-quantile of the data) to avoid an unequal filling of the numbers of rating classes to be analyzed by ordered logit. To begin with, I examine the full sample using the lnWARF and the average rating as asset pool quality measures. Control variables include the natural logarithm of the size of each deal, the LL and the SME dummy, the spread difference of BBB and AAA spreads on the CDO market at the time of the issuance of the deal, and the year of issue to capture the time dimension of the data. Results are displayed in table 4.5.[29] Starting with the univariate regressions, the coefficient on the lnWARF has the expected sign and is highly significant: a higher lnWARF, hence a lower asset pool quality, is associated with more differently rated tranches (model I). The same is expected to hold for the average rating: the coefficient should be negative given that a higher average rating indicates a better quality of the underlying assets. While the coefficient on the average rating is negative, it is not significant and the pseudo R^2 is zero. Model III includes the control variables only. All control variables are highly significant and of the expected sign. There is more tranching in larger deals, which is consistent with the results obtained in previous studies. Further, deals backed by leveraged loans and SME loans are tranched more than deals backed by bonds, CLOs, and CDOs. There is less tranching in case market conditions are severe, proxied by the difference in BBB to AAA spreads. And tranching increased over time, which is associated with increasing investor sophistication in line with the prediction made in Plantin (2004). Models IV and V include the control variables and the asset

[29] Sample size decreases to 798 observations as the number of rating classes cannot be derived for six deals. Further, there is no information on the deal volume for one deal.

Table 4.5: Tranching and pool quality – full sample – The dependent variable is the number of differently rated tranches. Results are reported for ordered logit estimation. Heteroscedasticity-robust standard errors are reported in parentheses. Significance of coefficients is indicated by asterisks, where ***, **, and * denote significance at the 1%, 5%, and 10% level, respectively.

	I	II	III	IV	V
	Coef. / se	Coef. / se	Coef. / se	Coef. / se	Coef. / se
lnWARF	0.463***			0.416***	
	(0.041)			(0.048)	
Average rating		−0.060			−0.251*
		(0.114)			(0.133)
Year			0.116***	0.126***	0.119***
			(0.033)	(0.032)	(0.034)
Ln deal volume			0.471***	0.492***	0.530***
			(0.076)	(0.076)	(0.086)
Spread BBB-AAA			−0.004***	−0.004***	−0.004***
			(0.001)	(0.001)	(0.001)
LL dummy			1.623***	0.949***	1.547***
			(0.189)	(0.195)	(0.192)
SME dummy			0.473**	0.576***	0.516***
			(0.185)	(0.183)	(0.185)
Sample size	798	798	798	798	798
McFadden's R^2	0.059	0.000	0.090	0.127	0.092
Prob > χ^2	0.000	0.601	0.000	0.000	0.000

pool quality measures. While the lnWARF again is highly significant, the average rating is now significant at the 10% level. In model IV it can be seen that adding the lnWARF reduces the coefficient on the LL dummy. The LL dummy thus appears not only to be a proxy for information asymmetries but proxies for asset pool quality as well, as already mentioned above. Even though the coefficient on the average rating now is weakly significant in model V, adding the average rating to the model does not significantly add explanatory power, while model IV has a pseudo R^2 of 12.7%. Tables 4.10 and 4.11 in appendix C show predicted probabilities from model IV for the number of differently rated tranches for several discrete values of lnWARF and of Spread BBB-AAA, holding the remaining variables at their means.

Several alternative model choices have been considered (not reported). Instead of using the difference in fitted BBB and AAA spreads I calculated moving averages of launch spreads on a 100 day (equal weighted) window by rating group, which allows me to capture more variation in launch spreads.[30] Results remain unchanged when using the difference in BBB and AAA moving averages of launch spreads. Further, results are robust to using any time series of spreads given that it is based on a sufficiently large data set (i.e. all but B spreads). As additional control variables, I include general bond market parameters such as the level and slope of the yield curve, with the level being the ten year zero rate and the slope being the difference of ten year and two year zero rates of government securities in the currency of the issue. While the level is not significant in any specification, the slope coefficient is negative and significant at 5% in models III and V and takes away some explanatory power from the spread difference. Inspecting the data reveals that the spread difference and the slope of the yield curve show a similar pattern over time, except for the last year of the sample period. Explanatory power remains virtually unchanged. Further, I integrated the average weighted average life (WAL) per deal. The average WAL is derived as the value weighted average of a deal's tranches' WALs, and is only available on a subset of 522 deals. Coefficients on the average WAL are positive and significant at 5% in models III and V, meaning a larger average WAL is associated with the creation of more differently rated tranches. A possible explanation can be that for a longer maturity of the tranches to be issued, the need to minimize spread payments by creating as many tranches as possible is enforced. Further, by adding the average WAL the coefficients on the spread difference and the year are significant at the 5% level only, the SME dummy loses significance, and the deal volume, the LL dummy, and the lnWARF remain unchanged.

I also run the same regressions on the number of market classes (not reported). The coefficients on the deal volume increase in size, which is consistent with the evidence presented in C/J. The number of market classes is affected more strongly by the deal volume, as market classes act as a 'buffer' in tranching. Given the hypothesis on tranching derived above, there might equally be a maximum threshold for tranche sizes. In case maximum tranche sizes are

[30] In case more than one tranche was issued on the same day in a given rating category, daily spread averages were used as an input for the moving average.

Table 4.6: Tranching and pool quality – univariate analysis of the small sample – The dependent variable is the number of differently rated tranches. Results are reported for ordered logit estimation. Heteroscedasticity-robust standard errors are reported in parentheses. Significance of coefficients is indicated by asterisks, where ***, **, and * denote significance at the 1%, 5%, and 10% level, respectively.

	spdef	spvar	Simulation	
			full letter	refined
Coef.	24.084*	34.026	1.145***	0.331***
se	(13.338)	(24.000)	(0.233)	(0.091)
Sample size	191	191	191	191
McFadden's R^2	0.014	0.008	0.062	0.050
Prob $> \chi^2$	0.071	0.156	0.000	0.000

reached, which is likely in case of large deals, tranches will be further partitioned into several same-rated tranches after the original tranching procedure. The coefficient on the LL dummy declines in significance, the SME dummy changes sign, the coefficient on the spread difference declines in size and remains negative, and the year no longer has an impact. The average rating is not significant in any specification, while the lnWARF is significant, again with a positive but smaller coefficient and a pseudo R^2 of only 0.7% in the univariate specification. Hence, based on the lnWARF, there is some weak support that lower quality deals are not only associated with more rating classes but equally associated with more market classes. An explanation could be that lower quality deals are more difficult to place, and that the creation of additional market classes facilitates the marketing of a deal. Overall explanatory power of the regressions is lower (highest in model IV at 4.7%).

The major weakness of the two quality measures lnWARF and average rating is that they both are based on the tranching of the deal and hence endogenous. In the following the subsample of 191 deals is analyzed where the S&P measures have been available. Both the S&P measures as well as the simulation results from section 4.4.3 are exogenous to the tranching of the deal, and can hence prove the robustness of the results derived on the full sample. I prefer to use the variability measure in the subsequent analysis and not the asset correlation parameter that I extracted for the simulation in section 4.4.3, as the parameter extraction of ϱ relies on assumptions and on the value of the default measure of the same deal. Given that the default and the variability measure are annualized values, their comparability across transactions is given. Furthermore, given that there are only eight deals having less than three differently rated tranches in the subsample, I reclassified them as having three differently rated tranches to avoid an excessively unequal distribution of the dependent variable in the ordered logit analysis.

To begin with, the number of differently rated tranches is analyzed in a univariate regression, using the S&P measures and the simulation results as independent variables. Results are presented in table 4.6. While all coefficients have the expected sign, the S&P variability measure is not significant and the S&P default measure is significant at 10% only. The results obtained when using the simulated number of differently rated tranches are stronger, with significance rising to the 1% level. The overall model fit is highest for the simulation based on the full letter rating scale, but comparably low in absolute terms. Table 4.12 in appendix C shows predicted probabilities for the number of differently rated tranches for different values of the simulated number of tranches based on the full letter rating scale.

Results change in the multivariate analysis presented in table 4.7. In the multivariate analysis, all control variables except the deal volume keep their sign and remain for the most part statistically significant. The lack of significance on the deal volume can partly be explained by the inclusion of the LL and SME dummies, as the deal size varies across these different types of underlyings, with SME transactions being by far larger than the remainder of the transactions. Deals back by leveraged loans and those backed by bonds or tranches of CLOs and CDOs are about the same size on average. Given this ordering, the positive coefficient on the LL dummy indicates that the LL dummy also seems to proxy for information asymmetries in the sense of Franke / Weber (2007). Concerning the pool quality measures, the S&P default measure is no longer significant when added to the control variables in model II, which is likely due to the inclusion of the leveraged loan dummy, as leveraged loans on average

Table 4.7: Tranching and pool quality – multivariate analysis of the small sample – The dependent variable is the number of differently rated tranches. Results are reported for ordered logit estimation. Heteroscedasticity-robust standard errors are reported in parentheses. Significance of coefficients is indicated by asterisks, where ***, **, and * denote significance at the 1%, 5% , and 10% level, respectively.

	I	II	III	IV	V	VI	VII	VIII	IX
	Coef. / se	Coef. / se	Coef. / se	Coef. / se	Coef. / se	Coef. / se	Coef. / se	Coef. / se	Coef. / se
Year	0.289*	0.301*	0.178	0.301*				0.256*	0.261*
	(0.150)	(0.179)	(0.165)	(0.173)				(0.149)	(0.146)
Ln deal volume	−0.188	−0.184	−0.196	−0.087				−0.972**	−1.044**
	(0.454)	(0.464)	(0.408)	(0.418)				(0.445)	(0.505)
Spread BBB AAA	−0.015***	−0.015***	−0.017***	−0.017***	−0.015***	−0.017***	−0.017***	−0.018***	−0.017***
	(0.003)	(0.003)	(0.004)	(0.004)	(0.003)	(0.004)	(0.004)	(0.004)	(0.004)
LL dummy	1.709***	1.794**	1.224***	2.608***	1.240*	1.147***	2.044**	1.146***	1.021**
	(0.412)	(0.713)	(0.411)	(0.851)	(0.710)	(0.420)	(0.797)	(0.427)	(0.402)
SME dummy	2.569**	2.554**	2.969**	3.115**	2.355***	2.756***	3.102***	3.142***	3.024***
	(1.220)	(1.252)	(1.248)	(1.267)	(0.802)	(0.850)	(0.909)	(1.145)	(1.155)
spdef		−3.354		−79.621*	22.274		−52.747		
		(26.519)		(44.844)	(21.801)		(38.089)		
spvar			56.113	130.464**		71.576**	129.354**		
			(34.820)	(61.089)		(29.811)	(55.248)		
Simulation full letter								1.400***	
								(0.321)	
Simulation refined									0.376***
									(0.121)
Sample size	191	191	191	191	191	191	191	191	191
McFadden's R^2	0.133	0.133	0.140	0.151	0.124	0.136	0.142	0.184	0.161
Prob $> \chi^2$	0.000	0.000	0.000	0.000	0.000	0.000	0.000	0.000	0.000

exhibit a higher default measure than the remainder of the data. Dropping the LL dummy from model II results in a highly significant positive coefficient for the default measure. The variability measure does not turn out to be statistically significant when added to the control variables in model III, either, yet it shows the expected positive coefficient and has a p-value of 0.107. In model IV, both the default and the variability measure are added together to the model. The variability measure now takes the expected positive coefficient, significant at the 5% level, while the default measure shows a negative coefficient, significant at the 10% level. A possible explanation of the unexpected sign on the default measure in model IV can be the high degree of collinearity in the default and the variability measure, as they exhibit a correlation coefficient of 0.89. For a further robustness check, the year and the deal volume are dropped from the analysis, as a Wald test cannot reject the hypothesis that these both factors are simultaneously equal to zero for models I-IV. Results are presented in models V-VII. While the default measure is not significant in models V and VII, the variability measure takes the expected positive coefficient in models VI and VII and is significant at the 5% level. Hence, there is some support that the correlation structure in the underlying asset pool has a stronger impact on the number of differently rated tranches than the average default probability. Concerning the simulated number of tranches, both coefficients are highly significant and positive, and overall explanatory power is highest for models VIII and IX. The deal volume now shows a significant negative coefficient in models VIII and IX. Given that the deal volume is an input parameter to the simulation procedure and is furthermore partly captured by the LL and SME dummies, and given that the impact of the deal volume is stronger on the number of market classes than on the number of differently rated tranches, a non-significant coefficient could be expected, yet the negative coefficient is puzzling.

As for the full sample, the average WAL, the difference in the moving average of CDO launch spreads, and general bond market characteristics have been included in the analysis (not reported). Only the inclusion of the level and the slope of the yield curve has an impact on the results presented in table 4.7. The ten year zero rate shows a positive coefficient, the slope parameter shows a negative coefficient with statistical significance ranging from not significant to highly significant for the different models, and the S&P measures lose their statistical significance. All other variables are not affected. Coefficients on the simulated numbers of tranches remain highly significant.

The number of market classes was analyzed for the small sample, as well. Here, only the spread difference shows significance for some model specifications with a negative coefficient.

Taken together, the univariate and multivariate analyses of the small sample in tables 4.6 and 4.7 confirm the results obtained on the full sample and hence confirm hypothesis one, in particular as the simulation implements just those mechanisms that are assumed to determine the number of differently rated tranches. Thus, a lower quality of the underlying asset pool leads to the creation of more differently rated tranches. Concerning the relative importance of the probability of default and the correlation of the underlying assets and hence the second part of hypothesis one, some support can be found that the number of differently rated tranches is affected more strongly by the variability measure in table 4.7. However, due to the collinearity in the S&P default and variability measure and the high levels of the default measure for leveraged loan transactions, the support for the second part of hypothesis one must be seen as only weak. Further, the highest overall significance is achieved by integrating the simulation results based on full letter grade ratings into the analysis. Hence, there is strong support that originators of CDOs maximize the number of differently rated tranches based on the full letter grade rating scale, but do not issue tranches that become too small to be marketable. This finding is in line with the mean of 3.82 differently rated tranches and the maximum number of eight differently rated tranches for the full dataset presented in table 4.2.

4.4.5 Empirical findings on the size of the junior and the senior tranche

In order to better disentangle the relation of asset pool quality and tranching, the size of the junior security and of the senior security are explored in this section, i.e. hypotheses two and three are examined. Both the relative size of the FLP as well as the relative size of the senior security are regressed (OLS) on the S&P measures; results are reported in table 4.8. I define the relative size of the senior security as the aggregate volume of all AAA-rated securities in each deal, standardized by the overall deal volume. Two deals that did not include AAA-rated securities are excluded from the analysis so that the relative size of the senior security is, for each observation, linked to the default threshold implied by an AAA rating.

Regressions I and II show that the relative size of the FLP is strongly affected by the average default probability of the underlying asset pool. The S&P default measure is highly significant with the expected positive coefficient and explains 41.7% of the variation in the data in the univariate specification (not reported). The S&P variability measure and its squared value are added to the model to examine the impact of the correlation structure in each deal on the choice of the size of the FLP, with the squared variability measure capturing a possible non-linear relation.[31] Neither of them is significant, and R^2 remains unchanged. As illustrated in section 4.3, an increase in ϱ is a mean-preserving spread of the distribution function for losses. The results obtained on the size of the FLP in table 4.8 indicate that the loss distributions for different values of ϱ do intersect at a loss rate that is about the size of the FLP. The effect of the steeper slope for the loss distribution for small loss rates and the stronger flattening thereafter cancel out, so that the variability measure does not have a significant impact on the size of the FLP. This result is in line with Franke / Herrmann / Weber (2007), who find that the "cumulative lognormal distributions, generated by different inter-industry correlations, intersect at loss rates which are only slightly smaller than the FLP"[32]. A second possible explanation for the lack of significance of the variability measure is that the sensitivity of the size of the FLP is larger towards changes in the average default probability than to changes in the asset correlation of the underlying asset pool. Hence, even though loss distributions might not intersect at a loss rate of about the size of the FLP for different values of the asset correlation, the impact of a shift in the loss distribution due to a change in ϱ on the size of the FLP is possibly dominated by the impact of the average

[31] Franke / Herrmann / Weber (2007) similarly include the reciprocal value of the diversity score in their analysis of the size of the FLP.

[32] See Franke / Herrmann / Weber (2007), p. 37.

Table 4.8: Junior and senior security and pool quality – The dependent variable is the relative size of the FLP (models I & II) and the relative size of the senior security defined as the relative size of all AAA-rated securities (models III & IV). OLS is estimated. Heteroscedasticity-robust standard errors are reported in parentheses below the coefficients. Significance of coefficients is indicated by asterisks, where ***, **, and * denote significance at the 1%, 5%, and 10% level, respectively.

	relative size FLP		relative size AAA	
	I	II	III	IV
spdef	2.344***	2.304***	-4.087***	-3.517***
	(0.457)	(0.496)	(0.701)	(0.813)
spvar	-0.258	1.169	-0.259	-18.891***
	(0.687)	(2.232)	(1.597)	(5.021)
spvar^2		-32.956		431.054***
		(47.711)		(99.858)
Sample size	191	191	189	189
Adjusted R^2	0.414	0.413	0.392	0.491
Prob > F	0.000	0.000	0.000	0.000

default probability. Regressing the relative size of the FLP on the variability measure only results in a positive coefficient on the variability measure with an R^2 of 32.5% (not reported). This supports the findings by Franke / Herrmann / Weber (2007) as it indicates a point of intersection of the loss distributions that lies within the FLP. However, due to the collinearity in the default and the variability measure, the variability measure likely proxies for the default measure in the univariate specification. Overall, H2 is strongly confirmed.

Concerning the size of the senior security, the default measure exhibits the expected negative coefficient and is highly significant in models III and IV. The impact of an increase in the variability measure, holding the default probability fixed, again depends on the point of intersection of the loss distributions given the change in the correlation structure. In a univariate regression (not reported), the variability measure shows a highly significant negative coefficient. Model III shows that when adding both the default and the variability measure to the regression, only the default measure exhibits statistical significance, which again underlines the importance of the default probabilities within the underlying asset pool for the tranching decision of securitization transactions. Model IV includes the default measure as well as the variability measure and its squared value. R^2 increases to 49.1% for model IV, and both the variability measure and the squared variability measure are highly significant. The generated function $-18.891\ spvar + 431.054\ spvar^2$ has its minimum at 0.0219, with 63% of the values of the variability measure in the data lying below the minimum. Hence, for a larger share of the data, the size of the senior security decreases with an increasing variability in the underlying asset pool. Dropping the default measure from model IV results in a minimum of 0.0279 for the generated function, with 74% of the values for the variability measure in the data lying below that minimum (not reported). These results are exactly in line with Franke / Herrmann / Weber (2007). They find that the size of the senior security increases with an increasing diversity score (hence better diversification) for large values of the diversity score. For small values of the diversity score, however the size of the senior security decreases with increasing diversification, just as the size of the senior security decreases with an increasing diversification (hence decreasing variability measure) for high values of the variability measure in the analysis presented here.

Overall, the size of the senior security decreases with a higher average default probability in the underlying asset pool and, for the majority of cases, increases with a rising diversification of the underlying asset pool. Hypothesis 3 is therefore confirmed. While Franke / Herrmann / Weber (2007) only analyze synthetic transactions and argue that "the TLP-size appears to be driven by the effects of the TLP on the originator's risk and return"[33] (with the TLP being the third loss position, which is used as a synonym for super senior securities), I argue that the effect is not specifically linked to synthetic transactions nor to specific originator motives, but simply due to the underlying financial engineering methodology inherent in tranching and the impact of changes in the pool quality on the shape of the loss distribution. However, the inverse relation of the size of the senior security and the degree of diversification for deals that involve a high variability of the loss rate for the underlying asset pool is puzzling and highlights the need for further research into this subject.

[33] See Franke / Herrmann / Weber (2007), p. 45.

4.5 Robustness of results

Several remarks need to be made regarding the robustness of the results. For the entire analysis, single-tranche deals have been excluded from the analysis as they are likely tailored to specific investor needs. Including single-tranche deals strengthens the results obtained on tranching for the full sample, while the results on the small sample are not influenced, as all deals where the S&P measures are available include more than a single tranche.

Methodologically, the number of differently rated tranches was analyzed by employing ordered logit. The parallel regression assumption inherent in ordered logit is violated for some model specifications, therefore several robustness checks were performed.[34] For the full model, the number of differently rated tranches, the dependent variable, was condensed to the values of two to five, so that deals containing only one differently rated tranche were considered to have two differently rated tranches, and deals that comprise more than five differently rated tranches were considered to have only five. This results in a comparably equal distribution of the dependent variable across these values. Using a Wald test by Brant (1990) shows that only the variable capturing the market conditions on the CDO market, the difference in BBB and AAA CDO spreads, causes the violation of the parallel regression assumption. Dropping the variable on the spread difference leaves the results on the remaining variables unchanged and the parallel regression assumption is no longer violated. Regarding the small sample analyzed in tables 4.6 and 4.7, the ordered logit analysis was reduced to a logit analysis as a further robustness check. As, for the subsample, the mean of the number of differently rated tranches is at 4.69 and the median at five, the dependent binary variable was set to the value of zero for deals that contain at most four differently rated tranches, and to the value of one for deals that contain five or more differently rated tranches. Results of the univariate regressions presented in table 4.6 are stronger for the logit specification, the coefficients on both the default and the variability measure are positive and significant at the 5% level, the coefficients on the simulated numbers of

[34] See Long / Freese (2003), pp. 165-168 for the parallel regression assumption.

tranches remain highly significant, and pseudo R^2 rises to at most 9.3% for the simulated number of tranches based on the full letter rating grades. Results for the multivariate analysis of the small sample are stronger as well, with e.g. the variability measure now also being significant at the 5% level in model III, and pseudo R^2 rising to at most 32.2% for model VIII.

As already mentioned above, there are some simplifications in the simulation procedure. A better fit of the simulated number of differently rated tranches and the true number of differently rated tranches could be achieved by taking into account cash flow modeling and hence specific credit enhancements. However, there is no data available on these transaction-specific structural elements. Further it is assumed that adjacent tranches that do not reach the threshold for their minimal size individually are not combined to derive one tranche that possibly reaches the threshold for the minimal size to be marketable. Such a decision would strongly depend on the motives of each transaction and is thus not integrated into the simulation. Also, varying maturities are not integrated in the simulation procedure. However, with the S&P measures being annualized figures, comparability across different transactions is given. Concerning the thresholds for the tranche sizes, using the 1%-quantile of the data is arbitrary. Therefore, the 5% and 10%-quantiles have equally been used in the simulation procedure, which gives rise to four additional possible combinations in the simulation process (5% vs. 10% threshold, refined rating scale or full letter grades only). Compared to the results obtained in tables 4.6 and 4.7, the results do not change substantially. Only the simulated number of differently rated tranches that is based on the 10% threshold and the refined rating scale loses statistical significance in both the univariate and the multivariate analysis; the coefficient still remains positive. This is due to the fact that the simulation based on the 10% thresholds for the tranche sizes and the refined rating scale results in only little variation in the simulated number of tranches, as most tranches do not exceed the threshold for their minimal size. Coefficients on the simulated number of differently rated tranches based on the full letter rating scale and the 5% as well as the 10% thresholds for the tranche sizes remain significant at the 1% level for both the univariate and the multivariate specification. Coefficients on the simulated number of differently rated tranches based on the 5% threshold for tranche sizes and the refined rating scale are significant at the 10% level in the univariate and at the 5% level in the multivariate specification.

As a last remark concerning the simulation procedure, I chose the tranching to be based on probabilities of default. While rating methodologies used by the different rating agencies differ, final ratings are rather homogeneous. For the 5055 tranches of the dataset, there are 2004 tranches that carry a rating by Standard & Poor's as well as by Moody's. Among these, there are 327 split ratings. However, 230 split ratings differ only by one rating notch (including refinements), 68 split ratings differ by two rating notches, and only 29 differ by more that two rating notches. Further, these differences in ratings are almost perfectly symmetric: 171 times the Moody's rating is better than the Standard & Poor's rating, while the opposite is true 156 times. Given there is no systematic pattern in the split ratings, any methodological choice for the simulation procedure and hence tranching based on probabilities of default is appropriate.[35]

For the analysis of the relative size of the junior and the senior security, OLS is a critical choice given the dependent variables are fractions bound between zero and one. Therefore, a generalized linear model according to Papke and Wooldridge (1996) using the binomial family and a logit link was used to verify the findings. Results for the S&P default measure are unaffected for both analyses. Concerning the variability measure, statistical significance at the 10% level is found in the analysis of the size of the FLP, which was not found using OLS. Marginal effects indicate that the impact of an increase in the variability measure on the size of the FLP is positive for small values of the variability measure, but negative for large values of the variability measure. However, as indicated by the deviance, the default measure explains almost all variation in the analysis of the size of the FLP. Regarding the size of the senior security, the variability measure is highly significant for the generalized linear model as well. Further, comparing the marginal effects evaluated at the means of the re-

[35] There are less ratings available from Fitch Ratings in the dataset. Comparing these ratings to those by S&P and Moody's equally exhibits a largely symmetric pattern of split ratings, with a weak tendency for Fitch ratings to be better.

gressors resulting from the generalized linear model to those obtained in OLS (model IV in table 4.8) does not reveal substantial differences.

4.6 Summary of results and discussion

In the above analysis a strong relation of asset pool quality and tranching of CDOs is found. Lower asset pool quality is linked to the creation of more differently rated tranches, which provides support for the transaction cost-based hypothesis on tranching. This result is in contrast to the prediction in Boot / Thakor (1993) and to the mixed empirical findings in Firla-Cuchra / Jenkinson (2005) on that relation. Different variables have been used to measure asset pool quality. The average rating is the weakest concept and adds only little explanatory power in the empirical analysis. The lnWARF, which captures the non-linear increase in risk that is associated with the tranching of any deal, can explain substantial variation in the data and shows the predicted coefficient in all specifications. Disentangling default probabilities and correlation by using the S&P measures 'default measure' and 'variability measure', there is some evidence that the impact of the correlation structure in the underlying asset pool has a stronger impact on the creation of differently rated tranches than the default probability. Contrary to the findings in Franke / Weber (2007), an increase in the correlation of the underlying assets is associated with the creation of more differently rated tranches. Using both the S&P default and variability measures as input parameters for a simulation on the number of differently rated tranches, further strong support is found for the transaction cost-based hypothesis on tranching. Results also indicate that originators maximize the number of differently rated tranches based on full letter rating grades. While the correlation in the underlying asset pool has a strong impact on the number of differently rated tranches, the size of the FLP is determined to a large extent by the average default probability of the underlying asset pool. The size of the senior security depends on both the average default probability and the correlation structure of the underlying asset pool. Overall, all three hypotheses, which were derived from the shape of the loss distribution, are confirmed in the empirical analysis. Additionally, it is found that actual CDO market conditions have a strong impact on the tranching decision, with higher levels of launch spreads on the CDO market implying the creation of less differently rated tranches. This finding is entirely new, as so far only general bond market conditions have been considered in empirical research, but not CDO market conditions. Taken together, there is strong support that tranching of CDOs is mostly based on financial engineering, and that transaction costs associated with high levels of spreads and small tranche sizes prohibit the creation of additional differently rated tranches.

Aside from transaction costs there is support for one of the major findings in C/J, namely that higher information asymmetries are associated with more tranching, as the LL and SME dummies show the appropriate sign. However, the LL and SME dummies equally capture information on the asset pool quality and on the deal volume. Given that C/J use a comparably weak measure of asset pool quality, the average rating, it would be interesting to verify the robustness of their proxy for information asymmetries across different asset categories (CMBS, RMBS, WBS, consumer ABS, etc.) by using more refined measures of asset pool quality. C/J proxy information asymmetries by ordering the different asset classes according to the variance of launch spreads. I am not able to pursue this additional verification as the data that is available to me only covers CDOs.

4.7 Conclusion

Given the high importance of the quality of the underlying asset pool on the tranching of CDO transactions, this chapter concludes with more general remarks on asset securitization. Models used by market participants and rating agencies are formally appealing and result in a mathematically precise determination of tranche sizes and corresponding ratings. In fact, this very precise modeling might have on the one hand suggested soundness of the estimates and on the other hand taken the focus away from an essential aspect in valuing securitization transactions, namely the proper calibration of input parameters such as probabilities of default and correlations. Taking the example of subprime mortgages, ex post the integration of higher default and correlation assumptions or stress scenarios seems to have been missing. Such assumptions however would have likely made the whole subprime segment and hence the originate-to-distribute business model unprofitable in the first place, as higher default and correlation assumptions would have led to higher refinancing costs due to substantially larger junior and mezzanine tranches, but smaller senior tranches. Given that the rating of structured products in the meantime strongly contributes to the revenues of rating agencies and that there is an oligopolistic market structure among rating agencies, one could suspect some degree of collusive behavior in the parametrization of securitization transactions that would merit closer examination. However, regulatory authorities did enforce the position of the rating agencies by strongly relying on ratings in the quantitative pillar of Basel II. Regulatory agencies might have to rethink whether they shall hold on to their bottom-up approach of regulation that is partly based on the judgment of privately organized, essentially unregulated rating agencies, or whether they shall more strongly focus on the detection of systemic deficits with a top-down approach.

Appendix for chapter 4

Appendix A: Mean-preserving spread of the loss rate distribution

For the large homogeneous portfolio, the distribution function for the portfolio loss rate is given by equation (4.1). Given an increase in ϱ to $\tilde{\varrho}$, the intersection of the distribution functions can be derived by setting

$$F_{p,\varrho}(x) = F_{p,\tilde{\varrho}}(x) \quad ,$$

which results in x^* given in equation (4.2). A proof that an increase in the asset correlation is a mean-preserving spread of the loss distribution can be derived by showing that $F_{p,\tilde{\varrho}}(x) > F_{p,\varrho}(x)$ holds for any $x < x^*$. Let this x be defined as $x^* - \Delta$, then, from equation (4.1),

$$\frac{\Phi^{-1}(x^* - \Delta)\sqrt{1-\tilde{\varrho}} - \Phi^{-1}(p)}{\sqrt{\tilde{\varrho}}} > \frac{\Phi^{-1}(x^* - \Delta)\sqrt{1-\varrho} - \Phi^{-1}(p)}{\sqrt{\varrho}}$$

must hold for the increase in asset correlation to be a mean-preserving spread. This relation can be written as

$$\Phi^{-1}(x^* - \Delta)(\sqrt{1-\tilde{\varrho}}\sqrt{\varrho} - \sqrt{1-\varrho}\sqrt{\tilde{\varrho}}) > \Phi^{-1}(p)(\sqrt{\varrho} - \sqrt{\tilde{\varrho}}) \ .$$

Bringing $\sqrt{1-\tilde{\varrho}}\sqrt{\varrho} - \sqrt{1-\varrho}\sqrt{\tilde{\varrho}}$ to the RHS depends on the sign of the term. The term is positive in case

$$\frac{\sqrt{\varrho}}{\sqrt{1-\varrho}} > \frac{\sqrt{\tilde{\varrho}}}{\sqrt{1-\tilde{\varrho}}} \ ,$$

which does not hold as $\tilde{\varrho} > \varrho$. Hence, as the term is negative, the equation can be written as

$$\Phi^{-1}(x^* - \Delta) < \frac{\Phi^{-1}(p)(\sqrt{\varrho} - \sqrt{\tilde{\varrho}})}{\sqrt{1-\tilde{\varrho}}\sqrt{\varrho} - \sqrt{1-\varrho}\sqrt{\tilde{\varrho}}} \ ,$$

which reduces to

$$x^* - \Delta < x^* \ ,$$

which is true. The same argument can be used to show that $F_{p,\tilde{\varrho}}(x) < F_{p,\varrho}(x)$ holds for any $x^* + \Delta$. Thus, an increase in the asset correlation implies a mean-preserving spread for the loss rate distribution.

Appendix B: Numerical mapping of ratings

Table 4.9: Rating indices and rating agencies' letter grades

Refined rating index	Rating index	S&P / Fitch	Moody's	Rating factor 10-year maturity
22	10	AAA	Aaa	1
21	9	AA+	Aa1	10
20	9	AA	Aa2	20
19	9	AA-	Aa3	40
18	8	A+	A1	70
17	8	A	A2	120
16	8	A-	A3	180
15	7	BBB+	Baa1	260
14	7	BBB	Baa2	360
13	7	BBB-	Baa3	610
12	6	BB+	Ba1	940
11	6	BB	Ba2	1350
10	6	BB-	Ba3	1766
9	5	B+	B1	2220
8	5	B	B2	2720
7	5	B-	B3	3490
6	4	CCC+	Caa1	4770
5	4	CCC	Caa2	6500
4	4	CCC-	Caa3	8070
3	3	CC	Ca	
2	2	C	C	
1	1	D	default	

Appendix C: Predicted probabilities for the ordered logit analyses

Table 4.10: Predicted probabilities for discrete changes in lnWARF – The following table presents predicted probabilities for the number of differently rated tranches derived from the ordered logit analysis of the full sample. For model IV of table 4.5 several discrete values of lnWARF are evaluated, while all other variables of the model (Year, Ln deal volume, Spread BBB-AAA, LL dummy, SME dummy) are held at their mean. The mean of the lnWARF variable is at five, which corresponds to a WARF of 148.4, which translates to an average rating in the range of A/A- for the chosen maturity of ten years. An lnWARF of two corresponds to a WARF of 7.4, which translates to a rating in the range of AAA/AA+. An lnWARF of eight translates to a WARF of 2981, which translates to a rating in the range of B/B-.

	$x=2$	$x=4$	$x=6$	$x=8$
$P(y=1 \mid x)$	0.1037	0.0479	0.0214	0.0094
$P(y=2 \mid x)$	0.2353	0.1345	0.0670	0.0310
$P(y=3 \mid x)$	0.3375	0.2940	0.1950	0.1063
$P(y=4 \mid x)$	0.1885	0.2596	0.2645	0.1984
$P(y=5 \mid x)$	0.1226	0.2360	0.3900	0.5227
$P(y=6 \mid x)$	0.0124	0.0280	0.0621	0.1321

Table 4.11: Predicted probabilities for discrete changes in Spread BBB-AAA – The following table presents predicted probabilities for the number of differently rated tranches derived from the ordered logit analysis of the full sample. For model IV of table 4.5 several discrete values of the difference in launch spreads of BBB and AAA-rated CDOs (Spread BBB-AAA) are evaluated, while all other variables of the model (Year, Ln deal volume, LL dummy, SME dummy, lnWARF) are held at their mean. The mean of the variable 'Spread BBB-AAA' is at 176.7 basis points, with a standard deviation of 64.64 basis points.

	$x = 100$	$x = 150$	$x = 200$	$x = 250$	$x = 300$
$P(y = 1 \mid x)$	0.0239	0.0289	0.0350	0.0422	0.0509
$P(y = 2 \mid x)$	0.0739	0.0876	0.1034	0.1213	0.1412
$P(y = 3 \mid x)$	0.2087	0.2332	0.2573	0.2800	0.3002
$P(y = 4 \mid x)$	0.2688	0.2727	0.2717	0.2660	0.2559
$P(y = 5 \mid x)$	0.3688	0.3312	0.2942	0.2587	0.2254
$P(y = 6 \mid x)$	0.0559	0.0464	0.0384	0.0318	0.0263

Table 4.12: Predicted probabilities for discrete changes in the simulated number of tranches – The following table presents predicted probabilities for the number of differently rated tranches derived from the univariate ordered logit analysis of the small sample with the simulated number of differently rated tranches based on the full letter rating scale as regressor (hence column 3 of table 4.6). The simulated number of tranches ranges from three to seven, the number of differently rated tranches in the small sample from three to six.

	$x = 3$	$x = 4$	$x = 5$	$x = 6$	$x = 7$
$P(y = 3 \mid x)$	0.8572	0.6565	0.3783	0.1622	0.0581
$P(y = 4 \mid x)$	0.0933	0.2029	0.2823	0.2202	0.1066
$P(y = 5 \mid x)$	0.0480	0.1360	0.3253	0.5744	0.7112
$P(y = 6 \mid x)$	0.0015	0.0045	0.0141	0.0431	0.1241

Bibliography for chapter 4

Bank of England (2007): Financial stability report, Issue No. 22, October 2007.

Bluhm, Christian / Overbeck, Ludger / Wagner, Christoph (2003): An introduction to credit risk modeling, London.

Boot, Arnoud / Thakor, Anjan (1993): Security design, in: *Journal of Finance*, Vol. 48, pp. 1349–1378.

Brant, Rollin (1990): Assessing proportionality in the proportional odds model for ordinal logitstic regression, in: *Biometrics*, Vol. 46, pp. 1171–1178.

Brennan, Michael / Hein, Julia / Poon, Ser-Huang (2008): Tranching and pooling, Working Paper, UCLA.

De Servigny, Arnaud / Renault, Oliver (2004): Measuring and managing credit risk, New York.

DeMarzo, Peter (2005): The pooling and tranching of securities: A model of informed intermediation, in: *Review of Financial Studies*, Vol. 18, pp. 1–35.

Fender, Ingo / Kiff, John (2004): CDO rating methodology: Some thoughts on model risk and its implications, Working Paper No. 163, Bank for International Settlements, Basel.

Firla-Cuchra, Maciej (2005): Explaining launch spreads on structured bonds, Working Paper, University of Oxford.

Firla-Cuchra, Maciej / Jenkinson, Tim (2005): Security design in the real world: Why are securitization issues tranched?, Working Paper, University of Oxford.

Franke, Günter / Herrmann, Markus / Weber, Thomas (2007): Information asymmetries and securitization design, Working Paper, University of Konstanz.

Franke, Günter / Weber, Thomas (2007): Wie werden Collateralized Debt Obligation-Transaktionen gestaltet?, in: *Schmalenbachs Zeitschrift für betriebswirtschaftliche Forschung*, Vol. 57/7 (Sonderheft), pp. 95–123.

Gaur, Vishal / Seshadri, Sridhar / Subrahmanyam, Marti (2003): Market incompleteness and super value additivity: Implications for securitization, Working Paper, Stern School of Business, New York.

Gibson, Michael (2004): Understanding the risk of synthetic CDOs, Working Paper, Federal Reserve Board.

Gorton, Gary / Pennacchi, George (1995): Banks and loan sales: Marketing nonmarketable assets, in: *Journal of Monetary Economics*, Vol. 35, pp. 389–411.

Hamerle, Alfred / Jobst, Rainer / Schropp, Hans-Jochen (2008): Rating von CDO-Tranchen – CDOs versus Anleihen: Risikoprofile im Vergleich, in: *Risiko Manager*, Vol. 22, pp. 1–14.

Hein, Julia (2006): Optimization of credit enhancements in collateralized loan obligations: The role of loss allocation and reserve account, Working Paper, University of Konstanz.

Krahnen, Jan Pieter / Wilde, Christian (2008): Risk transfer with CDOs, Working Paper, Goethe-University, Frankfurt a.M.

Löffler, Gunter / Posch, Peter (2007): Credit risk modeling using Excel and VBA, Chichester, West Sussex.

Long, Scott / Freese, Jeremy (2003): Regression models for categorical dependent variables using Stata, Texas.

Moody's Investors Service (2003): Moody's approach to rating synthetic CDOs, New York.

Moody's Investors Service (2005): Default and recovery rates of corporate bond issuers 1920-2004, New York.

Nomura (**2006**): Bond rating confusion, New York.

Papke, Leslie / Wooldridge, Jeffrey (**1996**): Econometric methods for fractional response variables with an application to 401(K) plan participation rates, in: *Journal of Applied Econometrics*, Vol. 11, pp. 619–632.

Plantin, Guillaume (**2004**): Tranching, Working Paper, Tepper School of Business, Pennsylvania.

Riddiough, Timothy (**1997**): Optimal design and governance of asset-backed securities, in: *Journal of Financial Intermediation*, Vol. 6, pp. 121–153.

Standard & Poor's (**2001**): New benchmarks overcome shortcomings of traditional CDO evaluations, New York.

Standard & Poor's (**2005**): CDO evaluator version 3.0: Technical document, New York.

Standard & Poor's (**2006**): CDO evaluator handbook version 3.0, New York.

Standard & Poor's (**2007**): Structured finance – commentary, New York.

Peter Lang · Internationaler Verlag der Wissenschaften

Donika Lilova

Bulgaria as a Target for Foreign Direct Investment

Frankfurt am Main, Berlin, Bern, Bruxelles, New York, Oxford, Wien, 2009.
XVI, 84 pp., 4 fig., num. tab.
European University Studies: Series 5, Economics and Management. Vol. 3335
ISBN 978-3-631-59361-5 · pb. € 19.80*

The book aims at providing an objective investment picture of Bulgaria. It is based on empirical criteria concerning the attractiveness of Bulgaria as a location for FDI. Additional task of the Thesis is the comparison of Bulgaria's political, macroeconomic and legal business environment, the production conditions and market opportunities with two successful Central European countries and with the neighbouring Romania. Part of the analysis included a comprehensive online survey with leading European entrepreneurs and investors. The author presents a well-weighted picture of the positive and negative factors of Bulgaria as a target for Foreign Direct Investment.

Contents: Foreign Direct Investment · Empirical criteria for choosing the right location for FDI · The Republic of Bulgaria · Foreign Direct Investment in Bulgaria · Factors determining the attractiveness for FDI · Empirical evaluation of Bulgaria as a target for FDI

MIX
Papier | Fördert gute Waldnutzung
FSC® C083411

Kolibri 360 GmbH
Ferdinand-Jühlke-Straße 7
99095 Erfurt, Deutschland
produktsicherheit@kolibri360.de